The Beauty of Algorithms: A Collection of AI-Generated Art

Field Du Boulay

Copyright © 2023 Field Du Boulay

All rights reserved.

ISBN: 9798378852147

DEDICATION

Dedicated to all the pioneers and innovators in the field of artificial intelligence, who have pushed the boundaries of creativity and imagination. Your tireless efforts has inspired us to see the world in new ways and to explore the limitless potential of AI-generated art. This book is a tribute to your vision and passion.

CONTENTS

1. **Introduction**
   - What is AI-generated art?
   - Why is it important?
   - A brief history of AI-generated art

2. **Algorithms, Deep Learning, and Neural Networks**
   - How do these technologies work?
   - What are the key techniques and processes used in AI-generated art?
   - Case studies of successful AI-generated artworks

3. **Examples of AI-Generated Art**
   - Visual art
     - Generative adversarial networks (GANs)
     - Style transfer
     - DeepDream

4. **Prompts and Techniques**
   - How do prompts work in AI-generated art?
   - What are some common techniques for generating prompts?
   - Examples of successful prompts and techniques

5. **Experimenting with AI-Generated Art**
   - Online tools and resources for creating AI-generated art
   - How to get started with creating your own AI-generated art
   - Tips and tricks for success

6. **Prompting creativity: AI-Generated Artworks**

7. **Prompt Engineering:**

8. **Challenges and Opportunities**
   - Ethical concerns around AI-generated art
   - Potential future developments in the field

- How AI-generated art is changing the creative landscape

9: **Conclusion**

- The potential of AI-generated art
- Key takeaways and final thoughts

10: **Exploring Further: Additional Resources for AI-Generated Art**

ACKNOWLEDGMENTS

I would like to thank my family for their unwavering support and encouragement throughout the writing process. Furthermore, I would like to thank the various online communities and resources that have helped me in my research and provided valuable insights into the world of AI-generated art.

INTRODUCTION

Artificial Intelligence (AI) has revolutionized many fields, including the world of art. AI-generated art has created a new wave of creativity and imagination, pushing the boundaries of what is possible. From paintings and sculptures to music and literature, AI-generated art has transformed the way we view and appreciate art.

In recent years, AI algorithms have become increasingly sophisticated, allowing artists to create stunning works of art with a level of complexity and intricacy that was previously impossible. Deep learning algorithms and neural networks can generate entire paintings or music pieces based on a single prompt or idea, resulting in unique and often unexpected creations.

While AI-generated art has generated excitement and interest in the art world, it has also raised ethical questions about the role of AI in the creative process. Some argue that AI art lacks the human touch and emotion that traditional art possesses, while others believe that it is simply a new form of artistic expression that should be embraced and celebrated.

In this book, we delve into the world of AI-generated art, exploring the various techniques and processes used to create these stunning pieces. From object-specific and style-specific prompts to mood-specific and randomized prompts, we explore the wide range of approaches used to generate AI art. We also showcase a collection of successful AI-generated artworks, highlighting the beauty and potential of this emerging field.

Whether you are an artist looking to experiment with AI-generated art, or simply an art lover interested in the latest trends, this book is the perfect introduction to the world of AI-generated art. Discover the beauty and potential of this new form of artistic expression, and explore the limitless possibilities of AI in art.

The Beauty of Algorithms: A Collection of AI-Generated Art

What is AI generated Art?

AI-generated art, also known as computational art, is a type of art that is created using artificial intelligence (AI) algorithms. These algorithms can be trained on large datasets of existing images, music, or other creative works, allowing them to learn patterns and generate new content based on that knowledge.

The resulting art can take many forms, including paintings, drawings, music, and even virtual reality experiences. AI-generated art can be created using various techniques, such as style transfer, where an algorithm applies the style of one image onto another, or generative adversarial networks (GANs), where two neural networks compete to create new images.

AI-generated art is an exciting new frontier in the world of creative expression, blurring the lines between human and machine creativity. It challenges us to think about the nature of art and creativity, and how AI can be used to augment or inspire human creativity. As AI technology continues to advance, we can expect to see even more innovative and breath-taking AI-generated art in the future.

Why is AI generated art important?

AI generated art is important for several reasons:

1. Advancing technology: The development of AI generated art is driving the advancement of AI technology. The more we explore the capabilities of AI algorithms in creating art, the more we learn about how these algorithms can be applied to other fields and industries.

2. Pushing creative boundaries: AI generated art is pushing the boundaries of what is possible in the world of art. It challenges traditional notions of creativity, authorship, and authenticity, and opens up new avenues for creative expression.

3. Democratizing art: AI generated art is accessible to anyone with a computer and an internet connection. It allows artists, designers, and creators from all backgrounds and skill levels to experiment with AI algorithms and generate their own unique works of art.

4. Inspiring new ideas: AI generated art can inspire new ideas and perspectives, providing a fresh take on familiar subjects and themes. It can also spark new conversations and collaborations between artists, scientists, and technologists.

5. Social and cultural impact: AI generated art can have a significant impact on society and culture. It can be used to explore important social issues and ideas, such as identity, representation, and bias. It can also reflect the values and beliefs of a society, and contribute to cultural trends and movements.

AI generated art has the potential to drive innovation, inspire creativity, and impact society in meaningful ways.

A brief history of AI-generated art

AI generated art has its roots in the field of computer graphics, which emerged in the 1960s with the development of the first computer graphics software. Early computer-generated images were basic and rudimentary, consisting of simple shapes and lines.

In the 1990s, new AI techniques such as neural networks and genetic algorithms began to be applied to art creation. One of the earliest examples of AI generated art was Harold Cohen's "AARON" program, which used AI algorithms to create abstract drawings and paintings.

In the early 2000s, the field of computational creativity began to emerge, focusing on the use of AI algorithms to generate creative works in various fields, including music, literature, and art. One of the most famous examples of this is the "The Painting Fool" by Simon Colton, which uses AI to generate realistic portraits and landscapes.

In recent years, AI generated art has gained mainstream attention, with the emergence of popular online platforms such as Deep Dream Generator and ArtBreeder. These platforms use sophisticated AI algorithms such as GANs and style transfer to create stunning and often surreal works of art, pushing the boundaries of what is possible with AI-generated art.

Today, AI generated art is a growing field, with artists, designers, and researchers exploring the possibilities of AI algorithms in creating new and innovative works of art. It is an exciting time for the intersection of art and technology, as AI-generated art continues to evolve and inspire new forms of creativity.

2 ALGORITHMS, DEEP LEARNING, AND NEURAL NETWORKS

AI-generated art relies on a variety of technologies, including algorithms, deep learning, and neural networks. These technologies are used to create complex systems that can recognize patterns and generate new content. The most successful AI-generated artworks often involve the use of multiple technologies in combination. For example, GANs can be used to create images that are almost indistinguishable from real photographs, while style transfer can be used to blend the characteristics of one image with another. Deep Dream uses a neural network to create surreal, dreamlike images.

Algorithms, Deep Learning, and Neural Networks are all integral to the field of AI generated art. In this chapter, we will explore how these technologies work and how they are used in creating art.

Algorithms

Algorithms are sets of instructions that are used to perform specific tasks. In the context of AI generated art, algorithms are used to create rules and parameters for generating art. For example, an algorithm might be used to determine the colour palette, brush strokes, or shapes used in a particular artwork. There are many different types of algorithms used in AI generated art, ranging from simple rules-based algorithms to more complex machine learning algorithms.

Deep Learning

Deep learning is a subset of machine learning that uses artificial neural networks to learn from data. Neural networks are modelled after the structure of the human brain, with layers of interconnected nodes that process information. Deep learning algorithms use these neural networks to identify patterns and relationships in data, and then use this information to make predictions or generate new data.

In the context of AI generated art, deep learning algorithms are used to analyze existing artworks and then generate new artworks based on what they have learned. For example, a deep learning algorithm might analyze a set of paintings by a particular artist and then generate new paintings in the same style.

Neural Networks

Neural networks are a type of machine learning algorithm that are modelled after the structure of the human brain. They consist of layers of interconnected nodes that process information in a hierarchical manner. Each node takes in input from other nodes, processes it, and then passes the output on to other nodes in the network.

In the context of AI generated art, neural networks are used to analyze and create images. For example, a neural network might be trained to recognize different objects in an image, and then used to generate new images that contain those objects. Neural networks can also be used to generate art in a specific style, such as the style of a particular artist or art movement.

Algorithms, deep learning, and neural networks are all key technologies used in AI generated art. They provide a powerful set of tools for artists and designers to explore new forms of creativity and expression, and are driving innovation in the world of art and technology.

What are the key techniques and processes used in AI-generated art?

AI-generated art is a complex field that combines many different techniques and processes. Here are some of the key techniques and processes used in creating AI-generated art:

Data Collection: AI-generated art relies on large amounts of data to learn and create new artworks. This data can come from a variety of sources, such as image databases, online galleries, or social media platforms. The data is used to train machine learning algorithms to recognize patterns and relationships in artwork.

Machine Learning: Machine learning is a subset of artificial intelligence that uses algorithms to learn from data. In the context of AI-generated art, machine learning algorithms are used to analyze and generate new artwork. For example, a machine learning algorithm might analyze a large number of paintings by a particular artist and then generate new paintings in the same style.

Generative Adversarial Networks (GANs): GANs are a type of machine learning algorithm that consists of two neural networks: a generator and a discriminator. The generator creates new images based on a set of input parameters, while the discriminator evaluates the quality of the generated images. The two networks are trained together, with the generator trying to create images that fool the discriminator into thinking they are real.

Style Transfer: Style transfer is a technique that involves taking the style of one image and applying it to another image. In the context of AI-generated art, style transfer can be used to create new artworks in the style of a particular artist or art movement.

Neural Style Transfer: Neural style transfer is a type of style transfer that uses deep learning algorithms to transfer the style of one image to another image. The algorithm analyzes both the content and style of the input images and then generates a new image that combines the two.

Evolutionary Algorithms: Evolutionary algorithms are a type of optimization algorithm that mimic the process of natural selection. In the context of AI-generated art, evolutionary algorithms can be used to generate new artworks by evolving a population of images over multiple generations.

These techniques and processes are used in various combinations to create AI-generated art. They provide artists and designers with a powerful set of tools for exploring new forms of creativity and expression, and are driving innovation in the world of art and technology.

Case studies of successful AI-generated artworks

1: The Next Rembrandt: In 2016, a team of data scientists, engineers, and art historians collaborated to create a new painting in the style of the Dutch master Rembrandt. They used machine learning algorithms to analyse Rembrandt's existing works, identifying patterns in his style, composition, and subject matter. They then used this data to create a 3D-printed painting that looks like a genuine Rembrandt. The painting, titled "The Next Rembrandt," was exhibited at the Mauritshuis museum in The Hague, Netherlands.

2: DeepDream: DeepDream is a project by Google that uses deep learning algorithms to create psychedelic and surreal images. The algorithm works by identifying patterns in existing images and then amplifying and repeating them to create new, abstract images. The resulting images often have a dreamlike quality, with swirling colors and distorted shapes. DeepDream has been used by artists and designers to create a variety of artworks, from posters and album covers to clothing and accessories.

3: AICAN: AICAN is an AI-generated art project by the artist and researcher Ahmed Elgammal. AICAN uses deep learning algorithms to analyze and generate new artworks, drawing on a database of images from different art movements and styles. The algorithm can generate new artworks in a variety of styles, from abstract expressionism to cubism to surrealism. AICAN has been exhibited in galleries and museums around the world, including the Art Institute of Chicago and the Guangzhou Triennial in China.

4: Portrait of Edmond de Belamy: "Portrait of Edmond de Belamy" is an AI-generated artwork created by the Paris-based art collective Obvious. The artwork was created using a GAN algorithm, which generated a new portrait based on a database of 15,000 portraits from the 14th to the 20th century. The final artwork was then printed on canvas and framed in a traditional style. In 2018, "Portrait of Edmond de Belamy" was sold at Christie's auction house for $432,500, making it the first AI-generated artwork to be sold at a major auction house.

These case studies demonstrate the range of possibilities and creative potential of AI-generated art. They show how AI can be used to push the boundaries of traditional art forms, explore new modes of expression, and create new forms of beauty and meaning.

3 EXAMPLES OF AI GENERATED ART

AI-generated art takes many forms, and in this section we will explore some of the most successful and inspiring examples. We will look at visual art created using GANs, style transfer, and DeepDream, and consider the music and literature created with neural networks and other AI technologies. The examples we discuss will offer insight into the creative potential of AI-generated art and the many possibilities for innovation in this field.

AI-generated art has come a long way since its early beginnings, and today there are a number of techniques and algorithms that are widely used to create stunning, one-of-a-kind artworks. In this section, we'll explore three of the most popular and widely-used techniques in AI-generated art: GANs, style transfer, and DeepDream.

1. GANs

    Generative Adversarial Networks (GANs) are a popular technique for creating AI-generated art. GANs use two neural networks: one network generates images, and the other network evaluates those images for their authenticity. The two networks work together in a feedback loop, with the generator network trying to create images that can fool the evaluator network, and the evaluator network trying to distinguish between real and fake images. This competition between the two networks results in the generator network creating images that are increasingly realistic and detailed.

    One of the most famous examples of GAN-generated art is the "Portrait of Edmond de Belamy" by the Paris-based art collective Obvious. The artwork was created using a GAN algorithm that generated a new portrait based on a database of 15,000 portraits from the 14th to the 20th century. The final artwork was then printed on canvas and framed in a traditional style. In 2018, "Portrait of Edmond de Belamy" was sold at Christie's auction house for $432,500, making it the first AI-generated artwork to be sold at a major auction house.

2. Style Transfer

    Style transfer is another popular technique in AI-generated art. Style transfer algorithms use deep learning to apply the style of one image to another image. The algorithm analyzes the style of the first image, and then applies that style to the second image, resulting in a new image that combines elements of both styles.

One of the most famous examples of style transfer in AI-generated art is the Prisma app, which uses a neural network to apply artistic styles to photos in real time. The app offers a range of different styles, from classic paintings to pop art to futuristic designs. Users can choose a photo from their camera roll or take a new photo, and then apply a style to it with a single tap.

3. **DeepDream**

DeepDream is a project by Google that uses deep learning algorithms to create psychedelic and surreal images. The algorithm works by identifying patterns in existing images and then amplifying and repeating them to create new, abstract images. The resulting images often have a dreamlike quality, with swirling colors and distorted shapes.

DeepDream has been used by artists and designers to create a variety of artworks, from posters and album covers to clothing and accessories. The algorithm has also been used in scientific research, helping to identify patterns and structures in medical images and other scientific data.

In conclusion, GANs, style transfer, and DeepDream are just a few examples of the many techniques and algorithms used in AI-generated art. Each of these techniques offers its own unique creative potential, and together they are helping to push the boundaries of traditional art forms, explore new modes of expression, and create new forms of beauty and meaning.

4 PROMPTS AND TECHNIQUES

Prompts and Techniques In order to create AI-generated art, an artist or researcher must provide a prompt for the algorithm to work from. Prompts can take many forms, from simple text strings to complex datasets. The prompts used in AI-generated art are carefully crafted to generate interesting and unique results, and the techniques used to generate them are a critical part of the creative process. In this section, we will explore the different types of prompts used in AI-generated art and provide examples of successful techniques for generating them.

How do prompts work in AI-generated art?

Prompts play a crucial role in AI-generated art. They are essentially the input that an artist provides to an AI model to generate an image. The prompts can be in the form of text, images, or a combination of both. AI models use these prompts to create original artworks that reflect the characteristics of the prompt.

For example, if an artist provides a prompt that says "a landscape with a sunset," the AI model will use this information to create an image of a landscape with a sunset. The AI model will analyse the prompt to identify the key features, such as the presence of a sun, the colour palette, and the overall atmosphere, and use this information to generate an image that fits the prompt.

The complexity of the prompts can vary, from simple textual descriptions to more complex inputs that involve multiple images or keywords. In some cases, artists may also provide specific constraints or parameters that the AI model should follow when creating the artwork. For example, an artist may specify the size of the canvas, the colour palette, or the types of elements that should be included in the image.

Prompts are essential in AI-generated art because they allow artists to guide the creative process while still allowing for the unpredictability and serendipity that comes with machine learning algorithms. They also help ensure that the final artwork reflects the artist's intent and style, even though it is generated by an AI model.

What are some common techniques for generating prompts?

There are several techniques that artists use for generating prompts in AI-generated art:

1. Text prompts: One of the most common techniques is to use textual prompts, where the artist provides a written description of the image they want to create. These descriptions can range from simple phrases, like "a landscape with mountains," to more complex sentences or paragraphs that provide detailed instructions for the AI model.

2. Image prompts: Another common technique is to provide an image as the prompt. The AI model can then use this image as a reference to create a new artwork that has similar visual characteristics.

3. Hybrid prompts: Some artists use a combination of text and image prompts to provide more detailed and specific instructions to the AI model. For example, an artist might provide an image of a flower along with a written description of the colour palette and composition they want to achieve.

4. Random prompts: Some artists use random prompts as a way to explore the creative potential of AI-generated art. For example, they may use a random word generator to provide prompts that are unexpected or unusual.

5. Interactive prompts: Some AI-generated art platforms allow users to interact with the AI model directly by manipulating the prompts in real-time. This allows artists to experiment with different prompts and see how the AI model responds to different inputs.

Examples of successful prompts and techniques

Here are some examples of successful prompts and techniques used in AI-generated art:

1. Text prompts: One successful example of using text prompts in AI-generated art is the "Birds AI" project by artist Cassie McQuater. McQuater provided a short description of a bird, such as "a bird with a green head and yellow belly," and used a GAN to generate a realistic image of the bird based on the description.

2. Image prompts: Style transfer is a popular technique for using image prompts in AI-generated art. One successful example is the "Starry Night" series by artist Vince McIndoe, where he used a neural network to apply the style of Vincent van Gogh's "Starry Night" to photographs of cityscapes and landscapes.

3. Hybrid prompts: The "Deep Dream" technique, developed by Google, combines image and text prompts to generate surreal, dreamlike images. Users can provide an image as the prompt and then choose a specific layer of the neural network to apply to the image, resulting in a unique and often surprising image.

4. Random prompts: The "GANbreeder" platform allows users to generate AI-generated art using randomly generated prompts. Users can choose from different categories, such as "fantasy creatures" or "abstract patterns," and the GAN generates unique images based on the selected

category:

5. Interactive prompts: The "Runway ML" platform allows users to interact with the AI model in real-time using a variety of prompts, including images, text, and sound. Users can experiment with different prompts and see how the AI model responds in real-time, making it a powerful tool for creative exploration.

The success of a prompt or technique in AI-generated art depends on the specific goals of the artist and the capabilities of the AI model being used. However, by experimenting with different techniques and prompts, artists can create unique and compelling works of art that push the boundaries of traditional art forms.

5 EXPERIMENTING WITH AI-GENERATED ART

Experimentation is at the heart of AI-generated art. One of the most exciting aspects of this field is the ability to explore new creative territories and push the boundaries of what we consider to be "art." In this chapter, we will encourage you to experiment with AI-generated art and provide some tips and techniques for getting started.

1. Start with simple prompts: If you are new to AI-generated art, it can be overwhelming to try and create complex images from scratch. Start with simple prompts, such as a basic description of a landscape or a few keywords that describe a specific emotion or feeling. This will allow you to become familiar with the process of generating art using AI without feeling overwhelmed.

2. Explore different platforms: There are many different platforms available for generating AI-generated art, each with its own strengths and weaknesses. Experiment with different platforms to find the one that best suits your creative needs. Some popular platforms include Deep Dream Generator, Artbreeder, and Runway ML.

3. Use multiple prompts: Many AI-generated artworks use multiple prompts to create complex and layered images. For example, you could use a text prompt to describe a landscape, an image prompt to provide a specific colour palette, and a sound prompt to influence the overall mood of the artwork. Experiment with different combinations of prompts to see how they affect the final output.

4. Collaborate with the AI: Instead of trying to control the AI model completely, try collaborating with it. Use the AI-generated output as a starting point and then make creative decisions based on what the AI has generated. This can result in unexpected and exciting artworks that would not have been possible through traditional methods.

5. Iterate and experiment: AI-generated art is a constantly evolving field, with new techniques and tools being developed all the time. Keep experimenting with different prompts and techniques, and don't be afraid to iterate on your previous works. By constantly pushing the boundaries of what is possible, you can create truly unique and ground breaking artworks.

Experimenting with AI-generated art is a fun and rewarding experience that can help you discover new creative possibilities. Whether you are an experienced artist or just starting out, there is always something new to discover in this exciting and rapidly evolving field.

6 PROMPTING CREATIVITY: AI-GENERATED ARTWORKS

The following pages contain a series of images generated by Mid Journey, a popular AI-generated art platform. Each image is accompanied by the prompts that were used to generate it, giving you an insight into the creative process behind AI-generated art.

Mid Journey is a powerful platform that uses a combination of algorithms, deep learning, and neural networks to generate stunning and complex images. It allows users to input prompts in various forms, such as text, image, or sound, and uses these prompts to generate unique and visually captivating artworks.

The images from beautiful landscapes to futuristic cityscapes and abstract art. Each image is accompanied by the prompts that were used to generate it, giving you an idea of how the AI model works and how different prompts can influence the final output.

By exploring these images and prompts, you will gain a deeper understanding of the creative potential of AI-generated art and how it can be used to create stunning and thought-provoking artworks.

The images presented in this book are just a small sample of what is possible with AI-generated art. there are countless styles, techniques, and possibilities that have yet to be explored.

One of the most exciting aspects of AI-generated art is its ability to constantly generate new and unique images. AI algorithms can be trained on a virtually infinite amount of data, allowing for an almost endless variety of artistic creations. This means that as AI technology continues to advance, we can expect to see an even greater diversity of styles and techniques emerge.

It's also worth noting that the images are a reflection of the prompts and data sets used to generate them. By tweaking the prompts or changing the data sets, entirely new sets of images can be created. This emphasizes the potential for personalized, customized art generated specifically for individuals or organizations based on their unique preferences and needs.

Prompt: Generate a portrait of a beautiful woman with long curly hair, wearing a floral dress and standing in a sunny meadow.

Output:

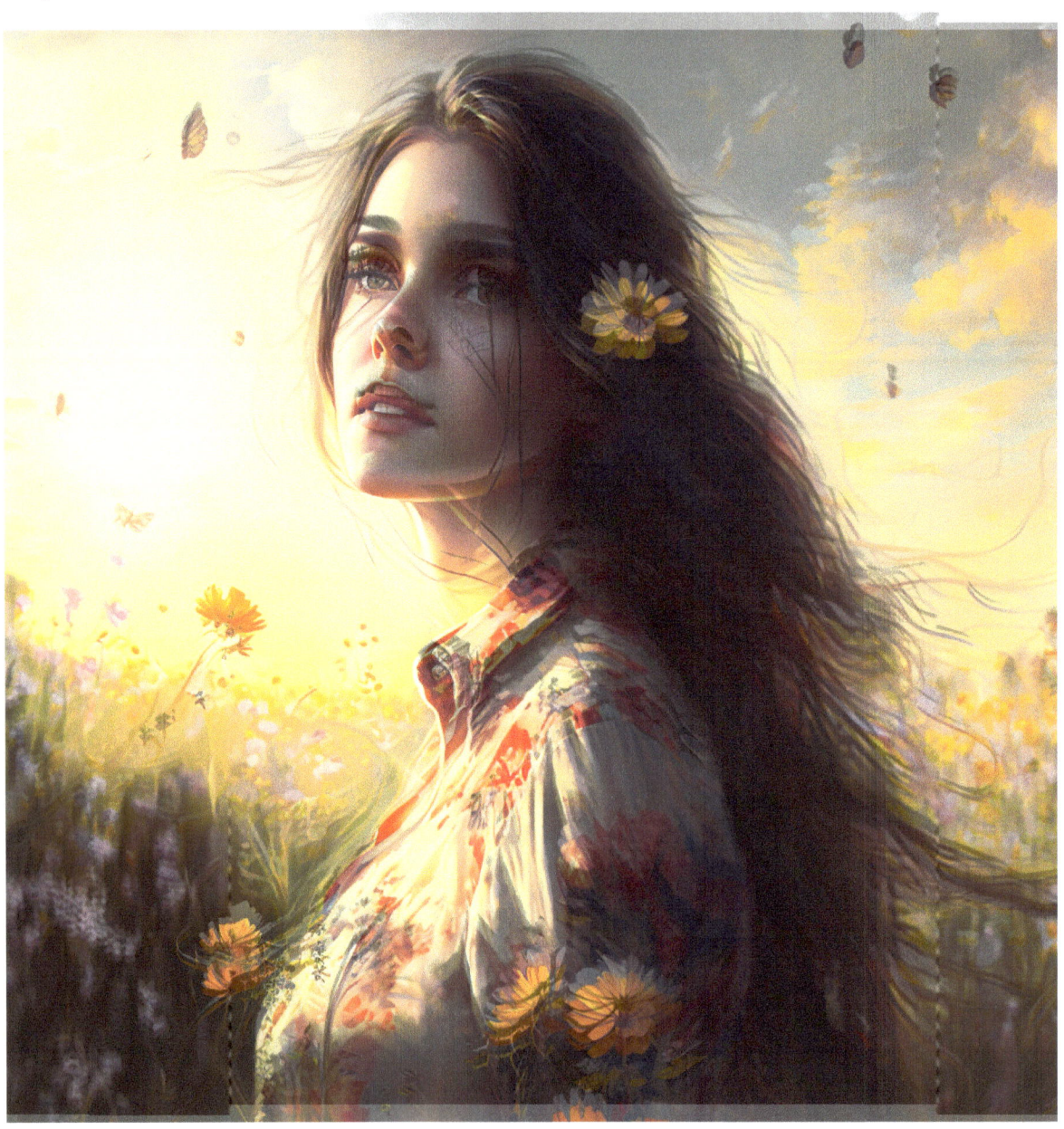

The Beauty of Algorithms: A Collection of AI-Generated Art

Prompt: Create an image of a beautiful woman with piercing blue eyes and an enigmatic smile, surrounded by a field of wildflowers.

Output:

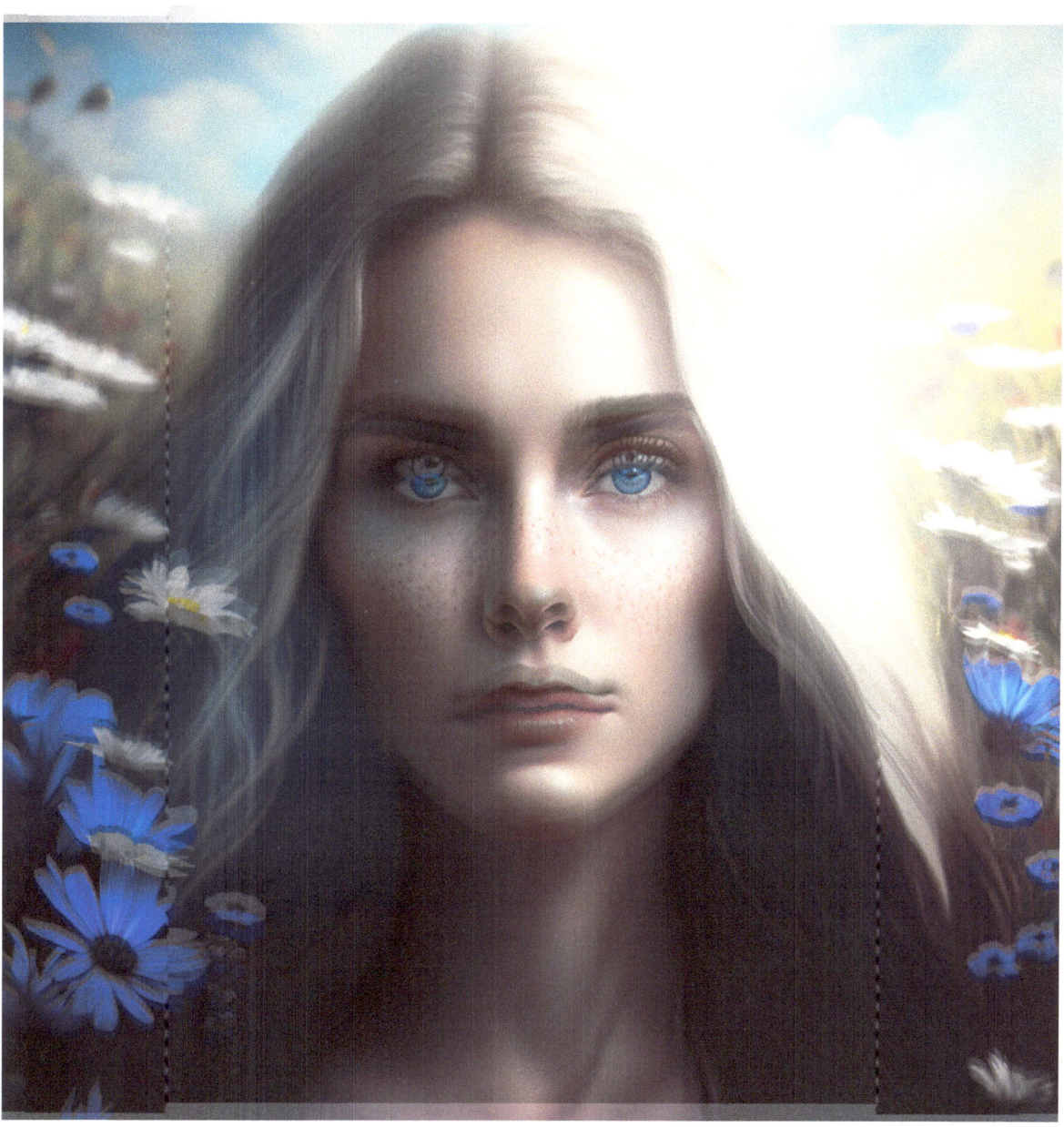

Prompt: Generate a portrait of a young woman with soft features and delicate bone structure, wearing a flowing white dress and standing in front of a misty forest.

Output:

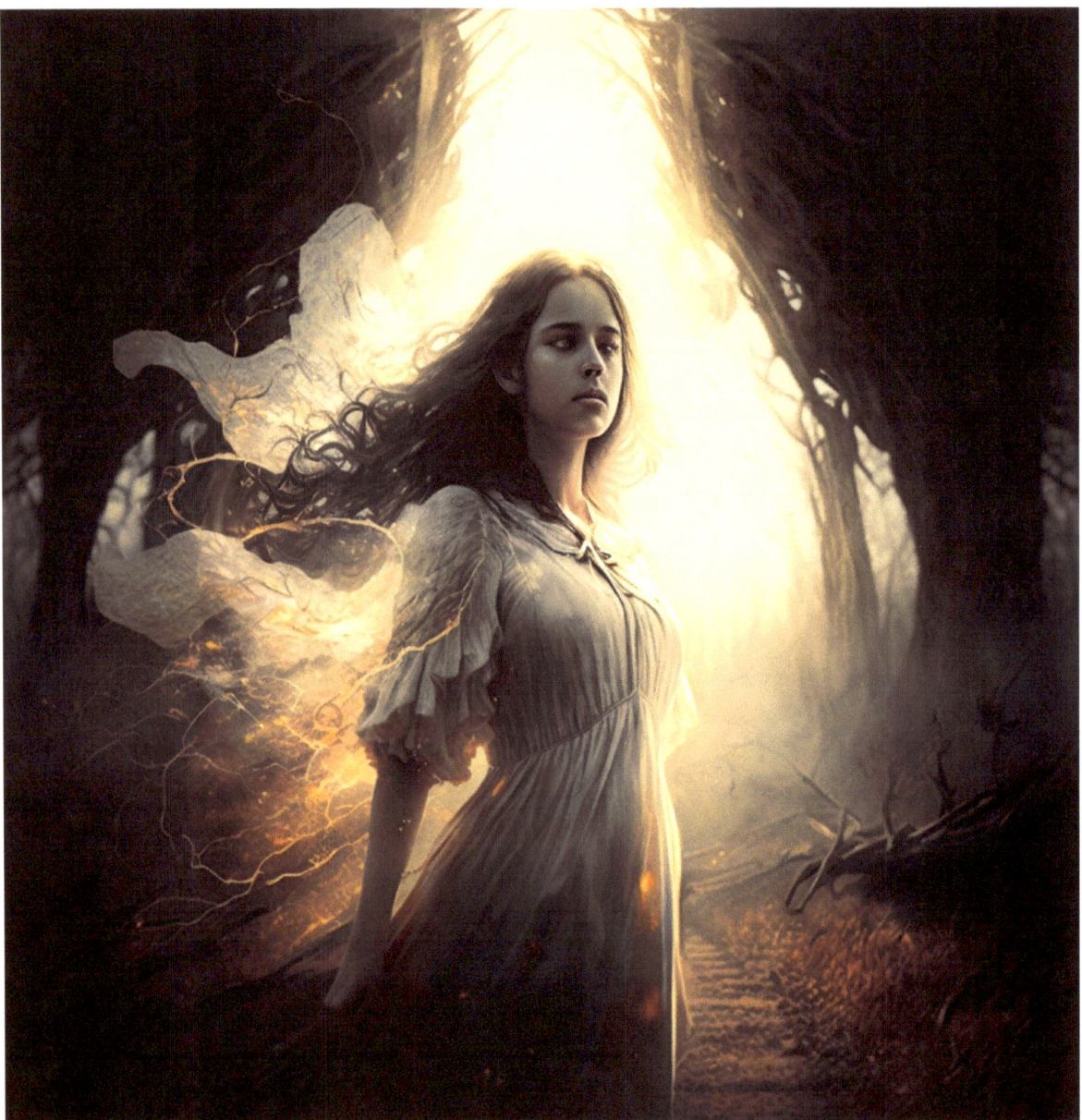

Prompt: Create an image of a beautiful woman with dark hair and almond-shaped eyes, wearing a red evening gown and standing on the balcony of a grand mansion.

Output:

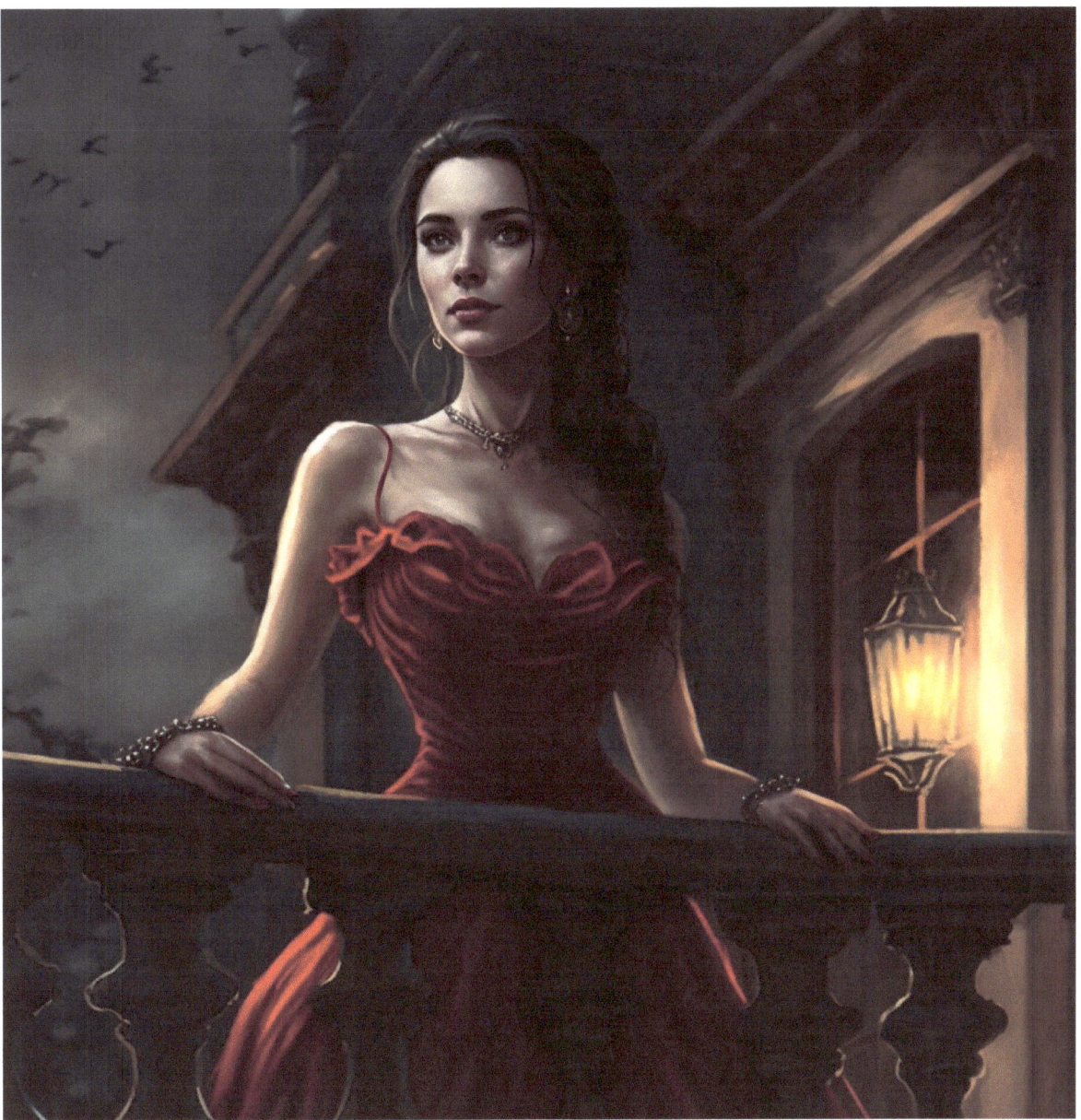

Prompt: Generate a portrait of a beautiful woman with high cheekbones and a wide smile, wearing a brightly coloured scarf and standing on a beach at sunset.

Output:

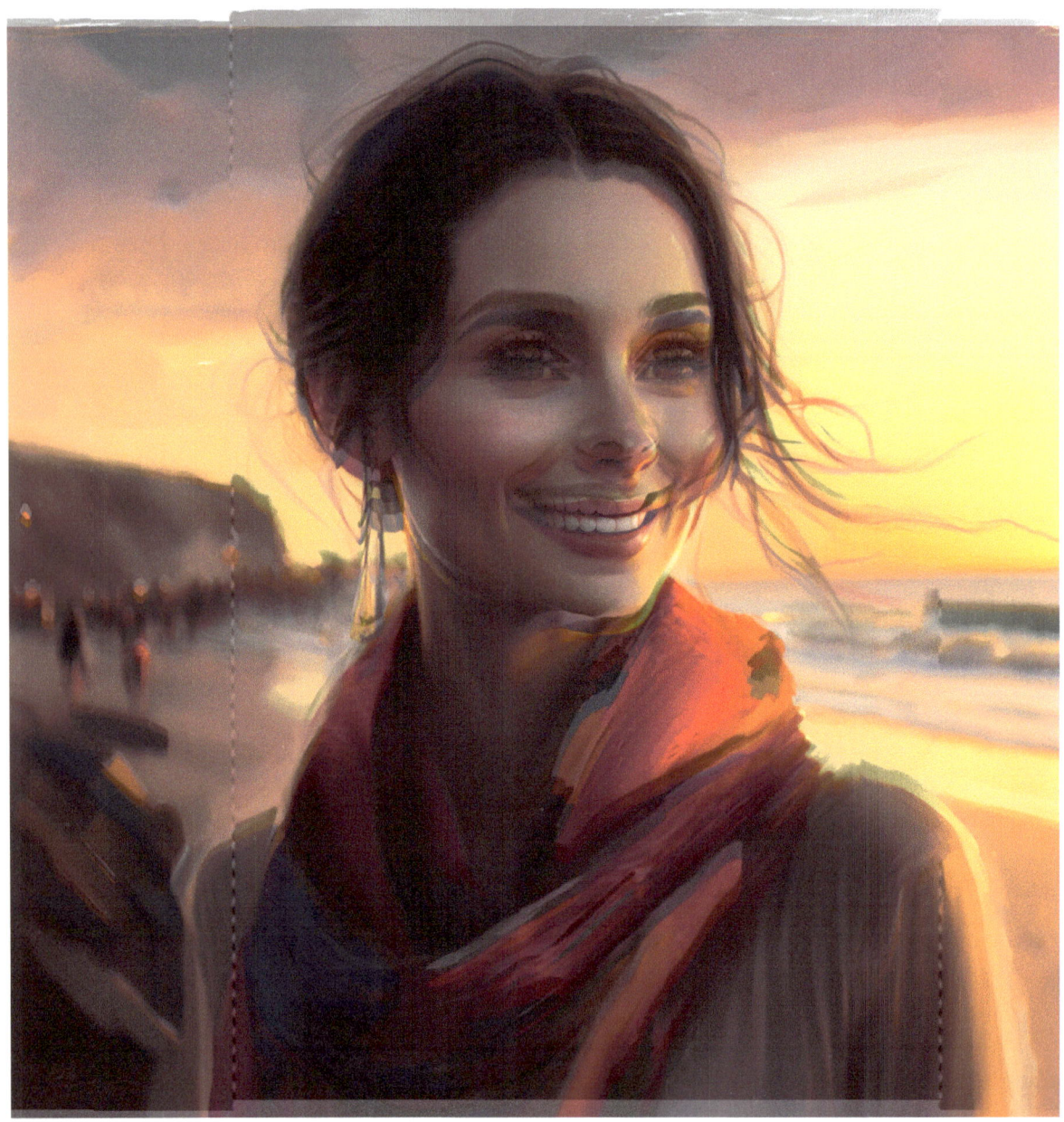

Prompt: Generate an image of a serene mountain lake surrounded by evergreen trees and snow-capped peaks in the distance.

Output:

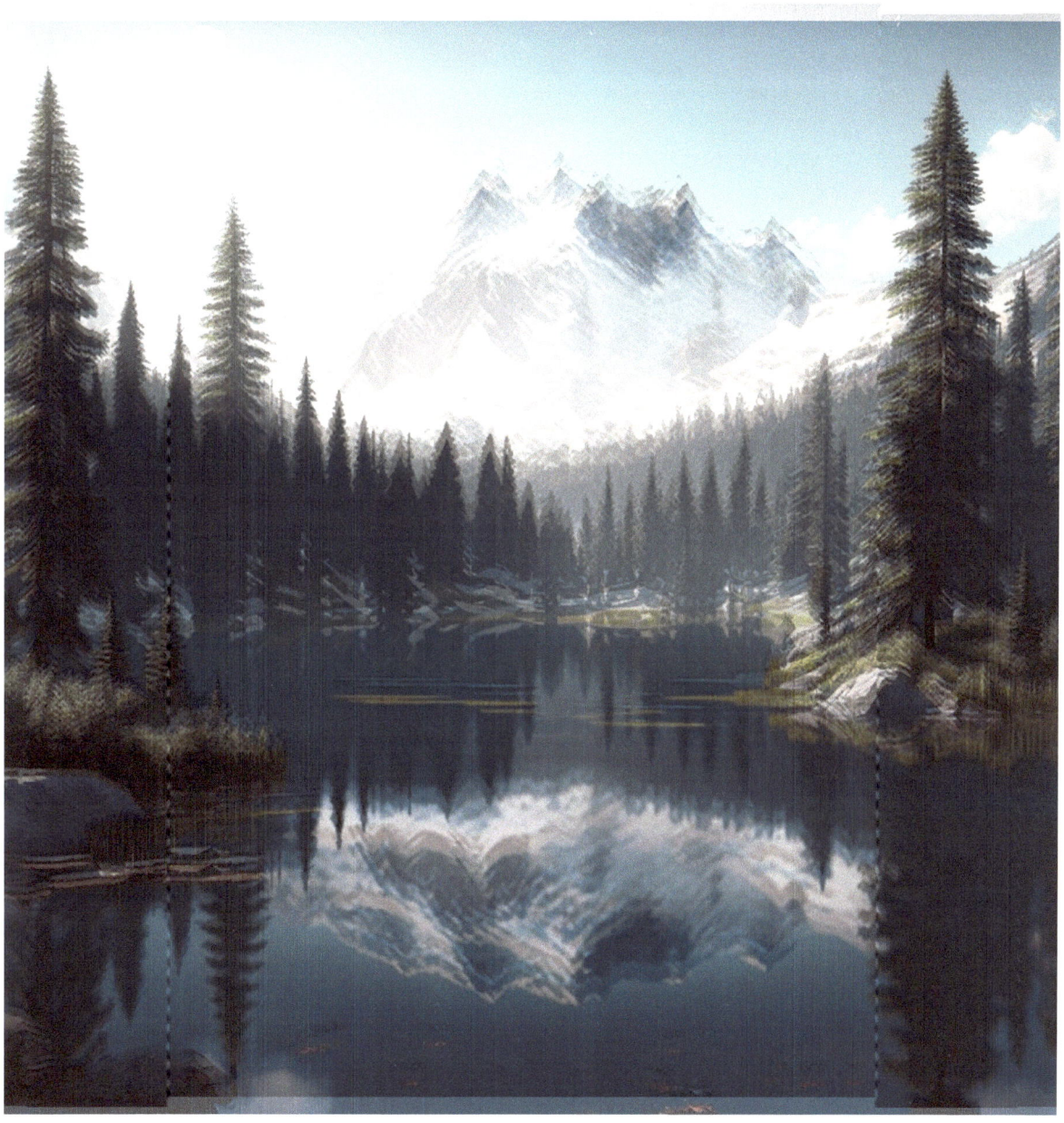

Prompt: Create a scene of a peaceful countryside with golden fields of wheat, gently rolling hills, and a clear blue sky.

Output:

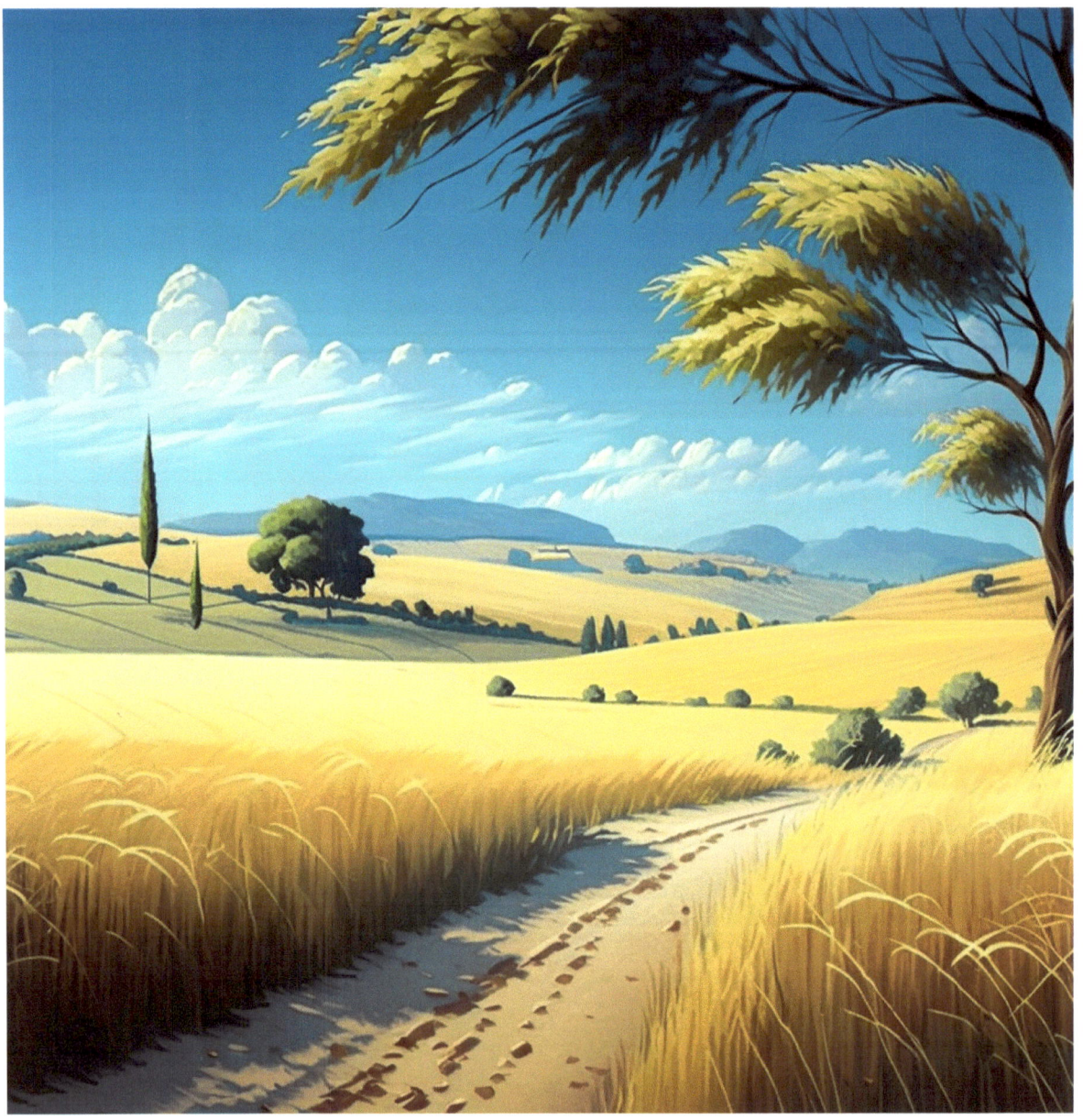

Prompt: Generate a misty, magical forest with tall, twisted trees and shafts of sunlight filtering through the branches.

Output:

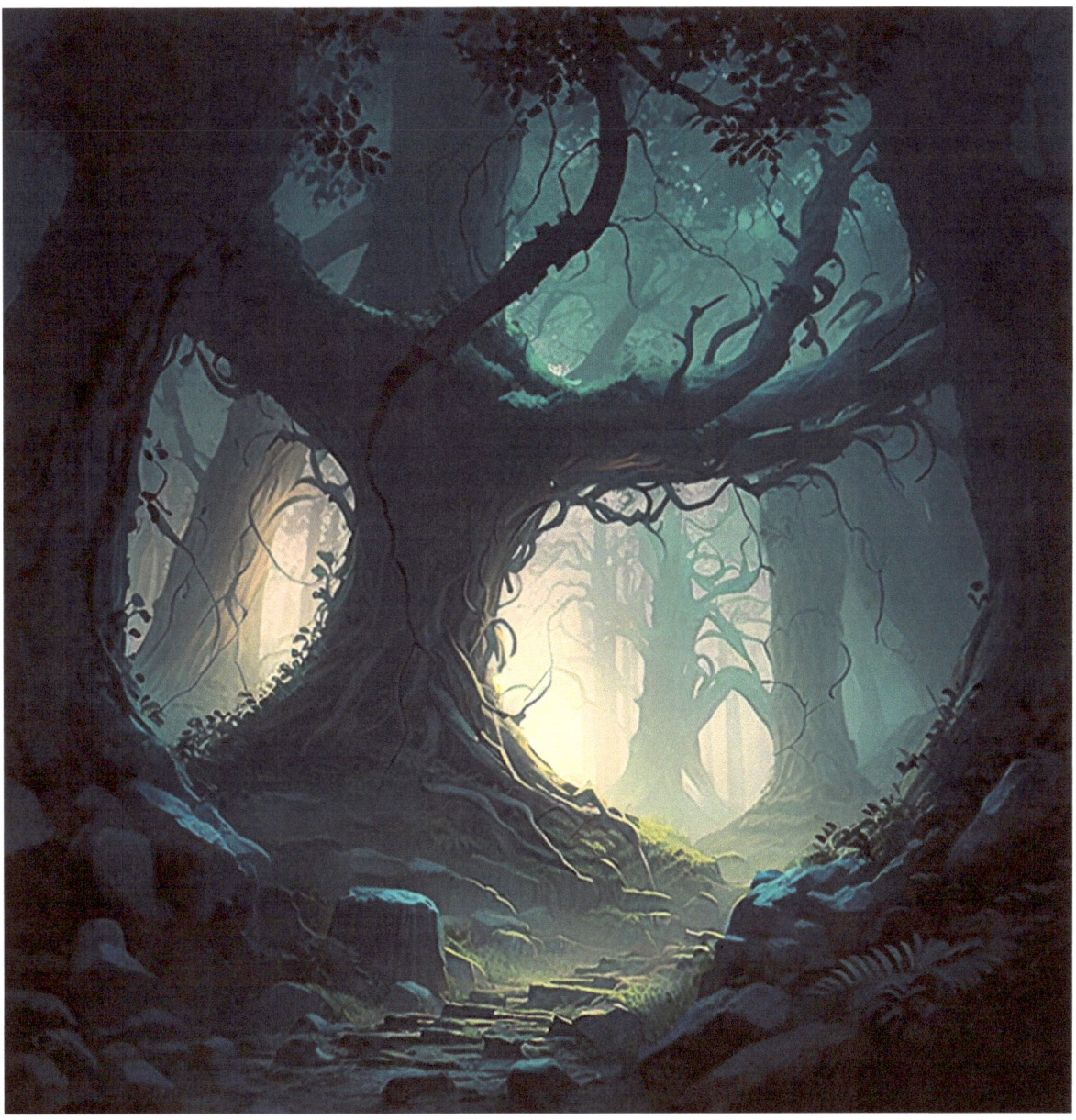

Prompt: Create an image of a tranquil ocean beach at sunset, with waves gently lapping at the shore and seagulls in the distance.

Output:

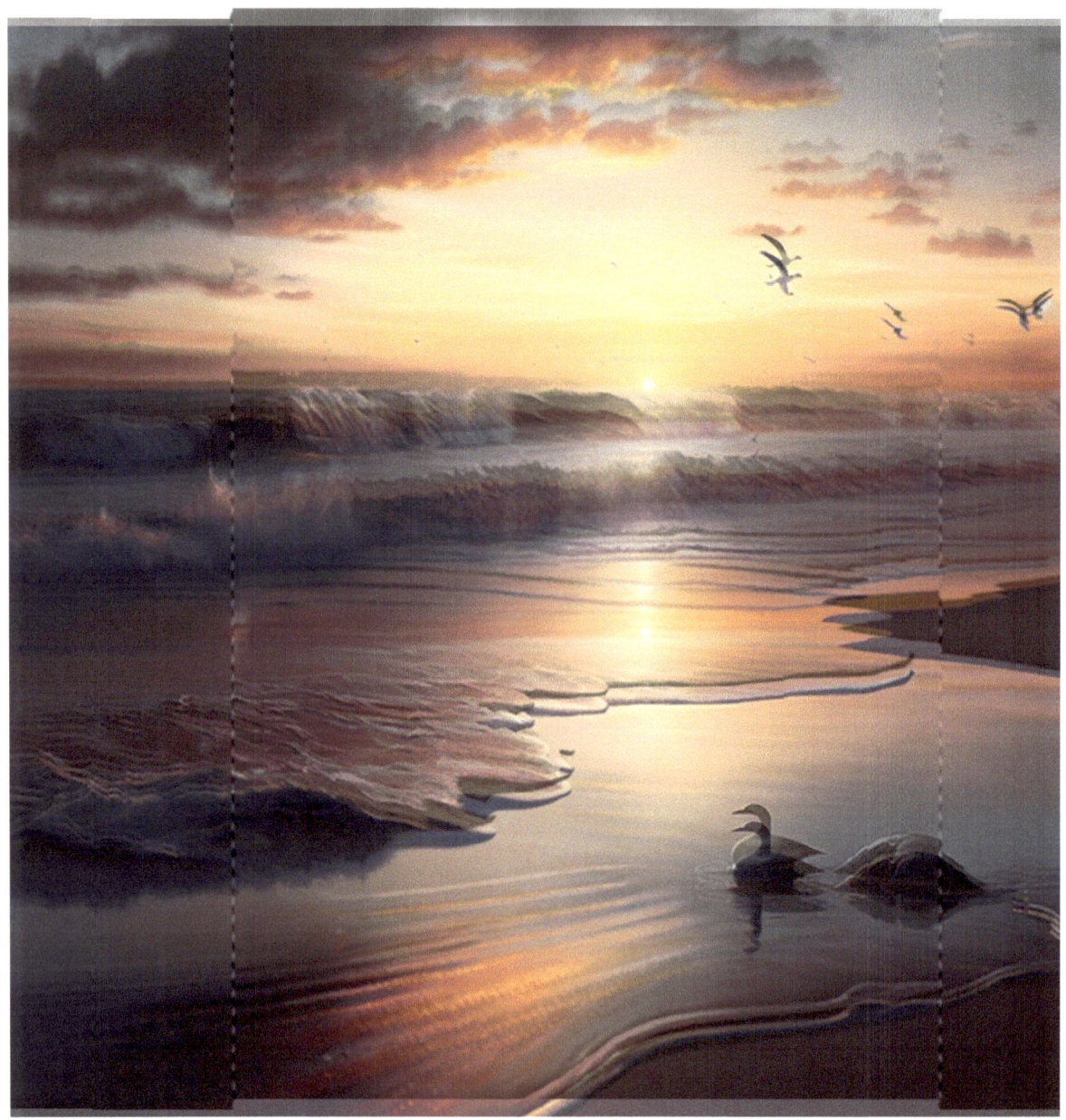

Prompt: Generate a vast, alien desert with towering sand dunes and strange rock formations, under a sky filled with strange stars.

Output:

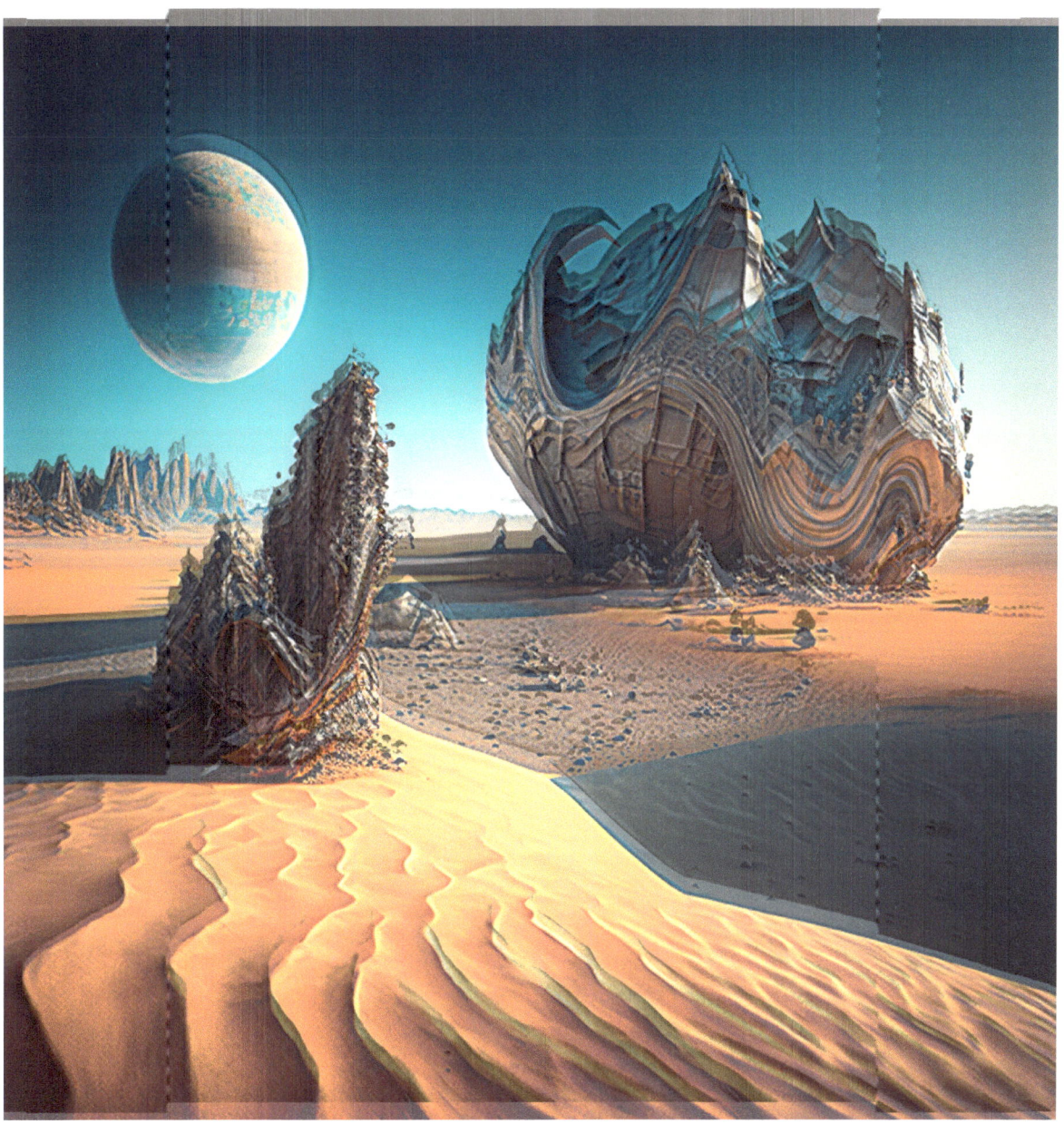

Prompt: Generate a desert scene in the style of Salvador Dali.

Output:

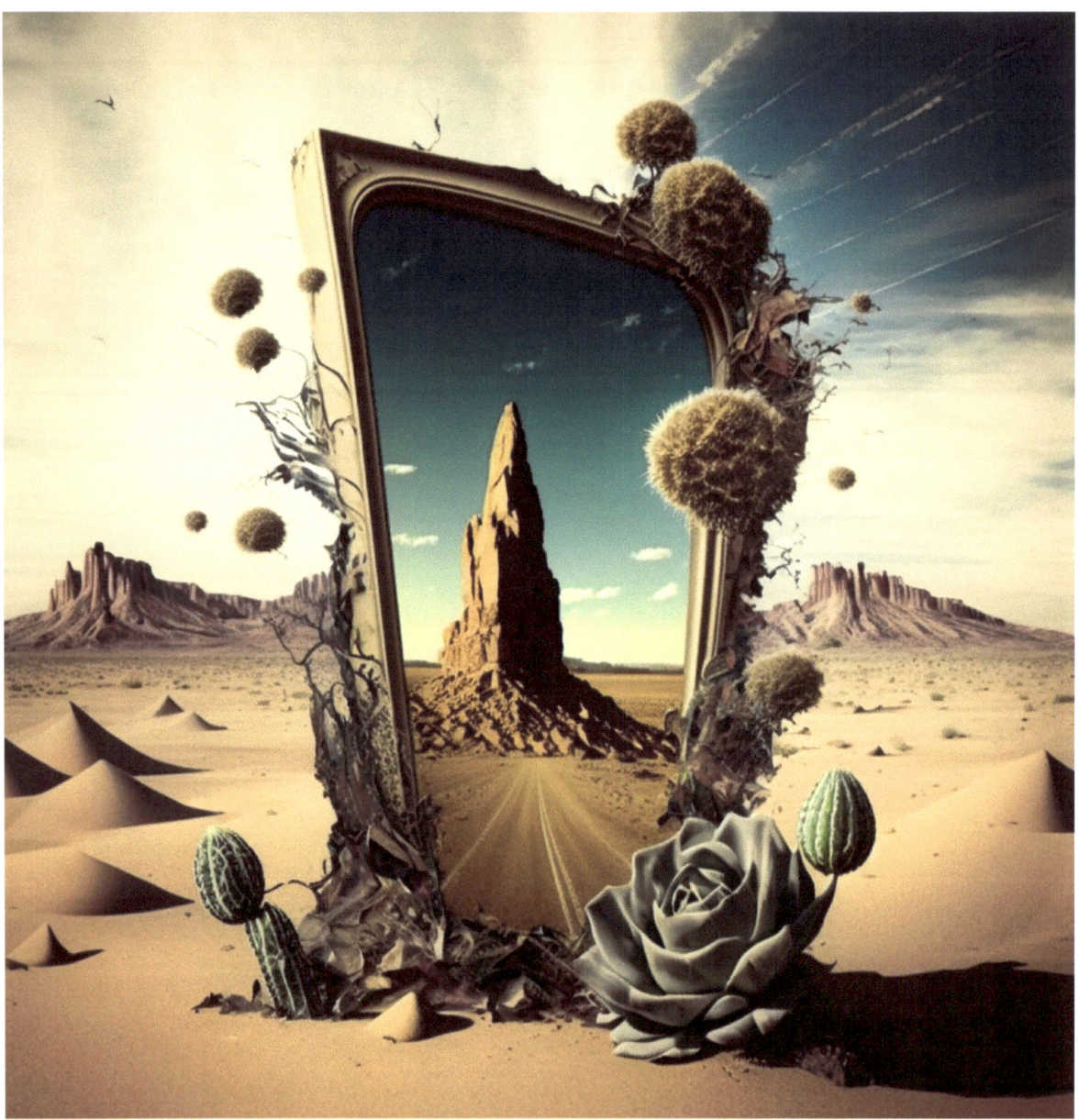

Prompt: Create a picture of Pablo Picasso in the style of Pablo Picasso.

Output:

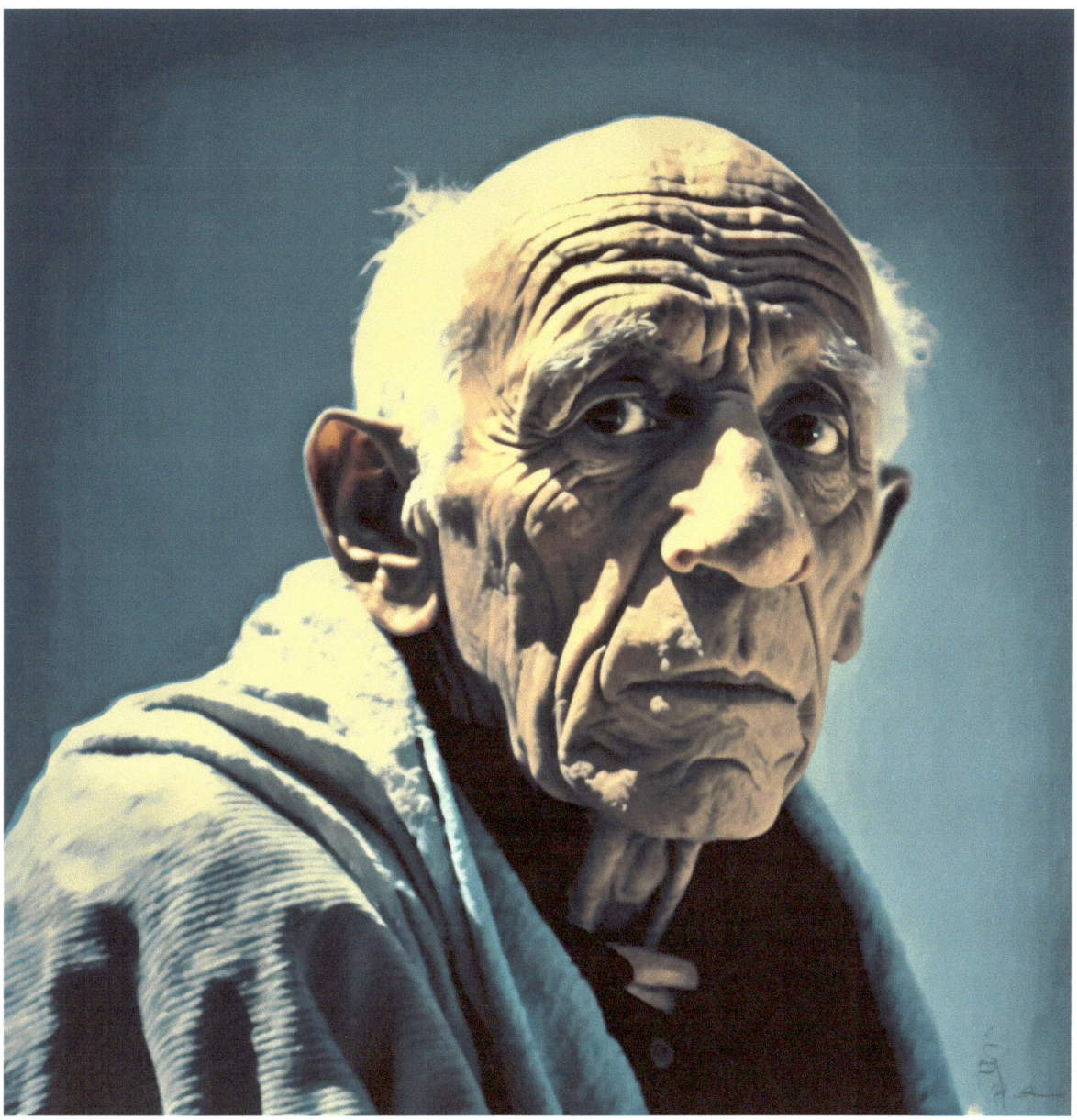

Prompt: A multi colored jeweled Chameleon detailed, hyper realistic beautiful

Output:

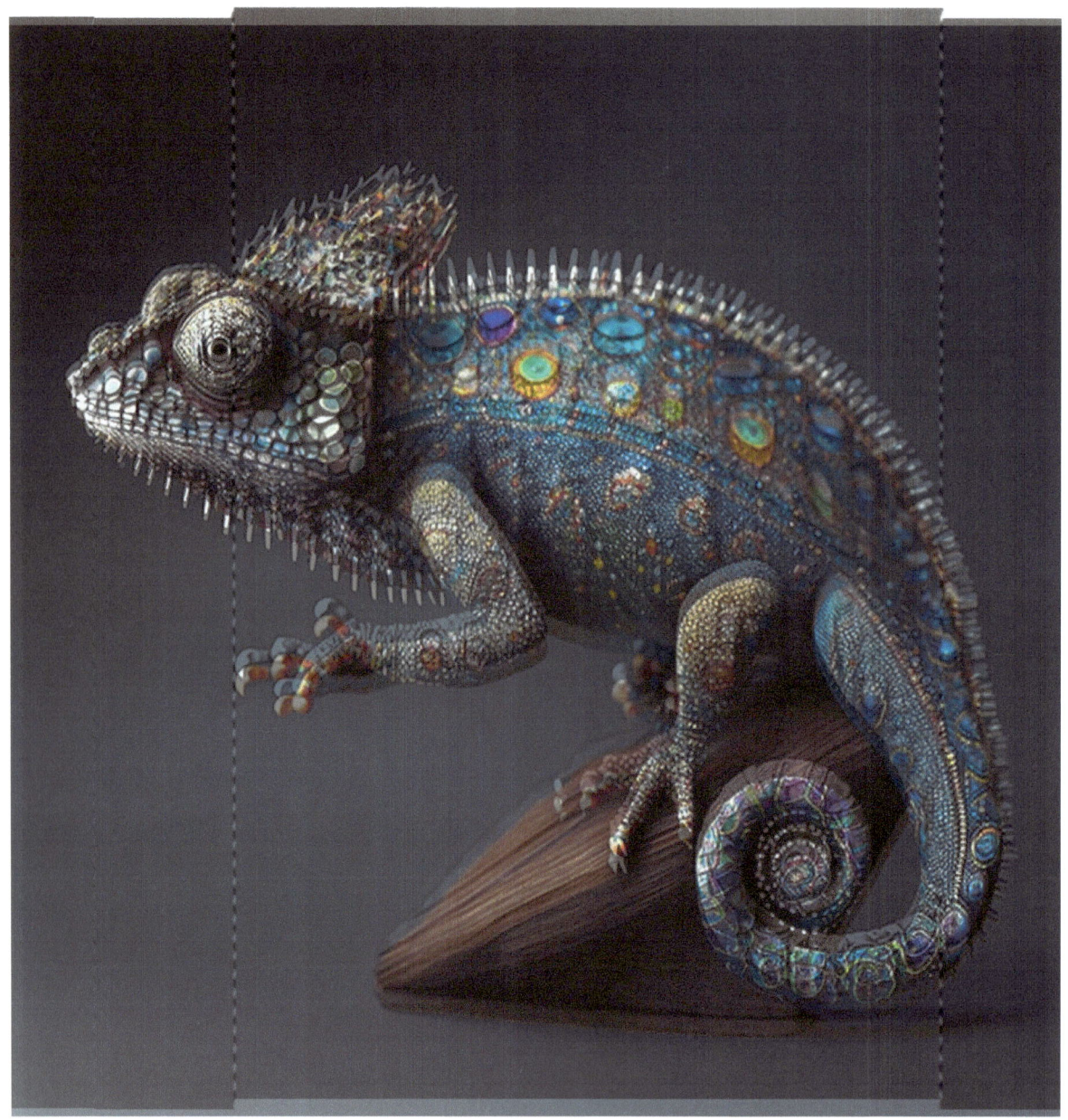

Prompt: Create an image of a castle on a hill, surrounded by a moat filled with dragons, with a magical rainbow in the sky.

Output:

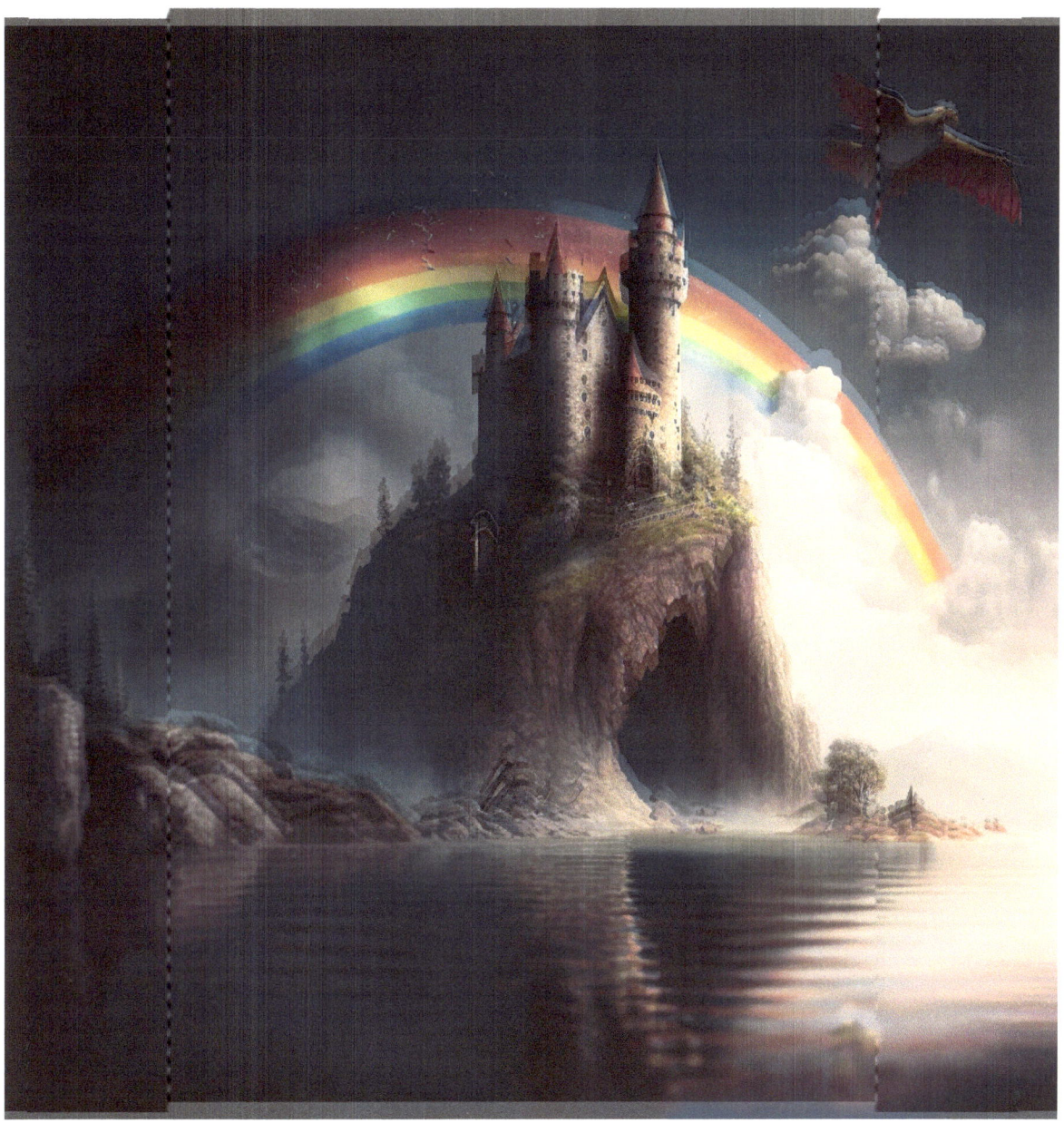

Prompt: Generate a scene of a fairy glade, with shimmering butterfly wings and fireflies dancing around a glittering pool of water.

Output:

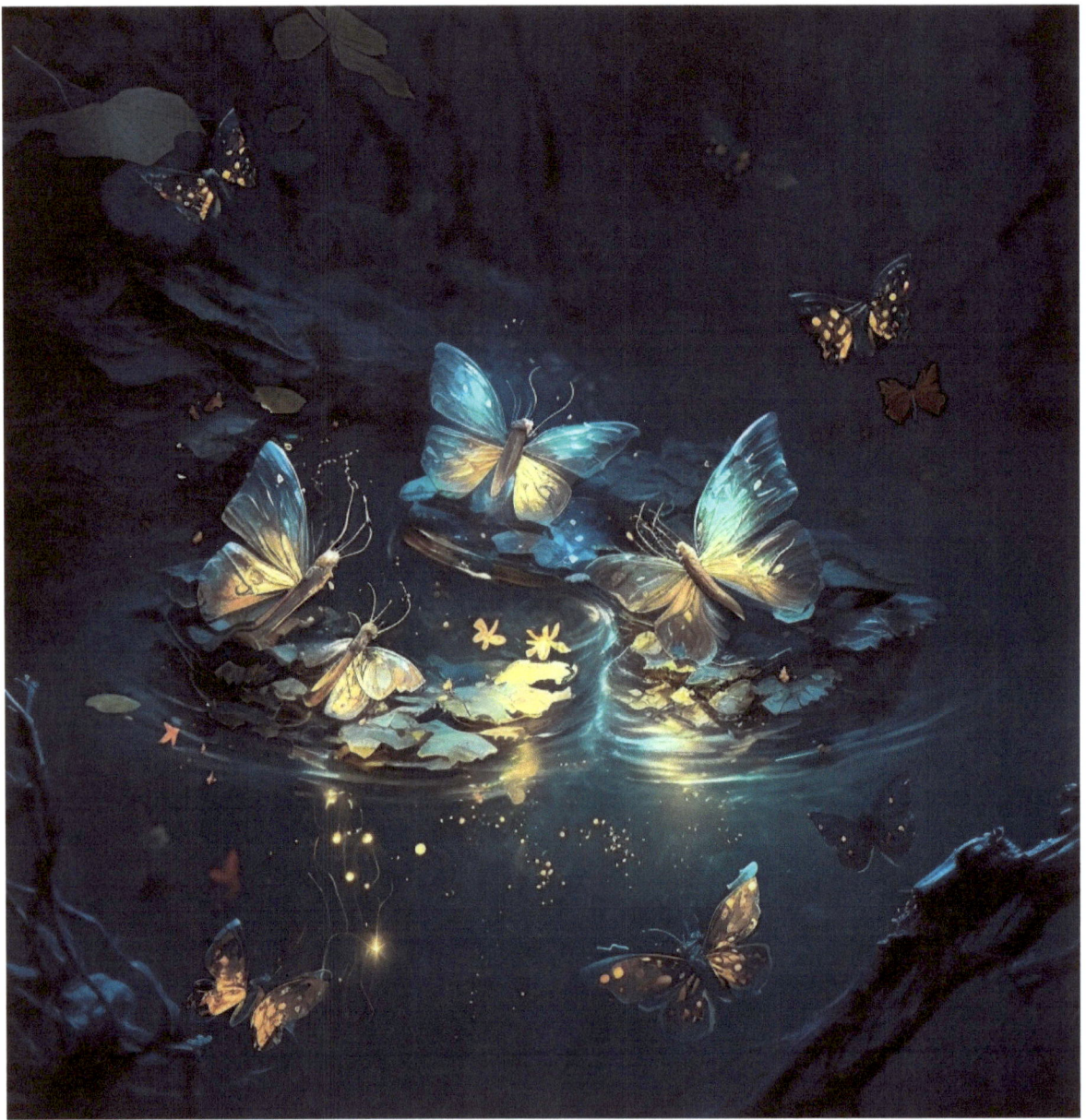

Prompt: Create an image of a magical marketplace in a sprawling, exotic city, with vendors selling potions, enchanted jewelry, and mythical creatures.

Output:

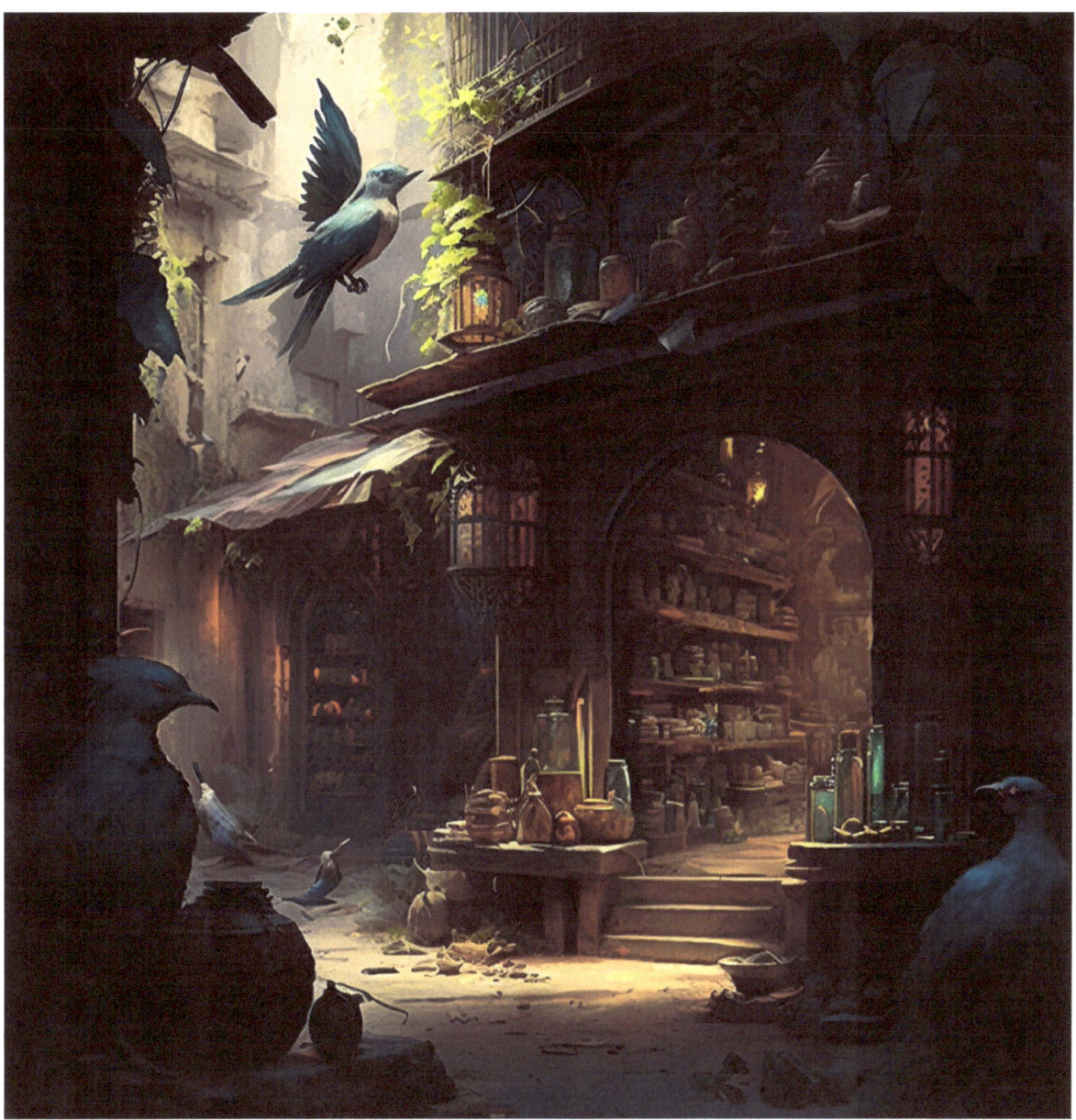

Prompt: Generate a portrait of a majestic unicorn, standing in a clearing in a dense, enchanted forest, with shafts of sunlight filtering through the trees.

Output:

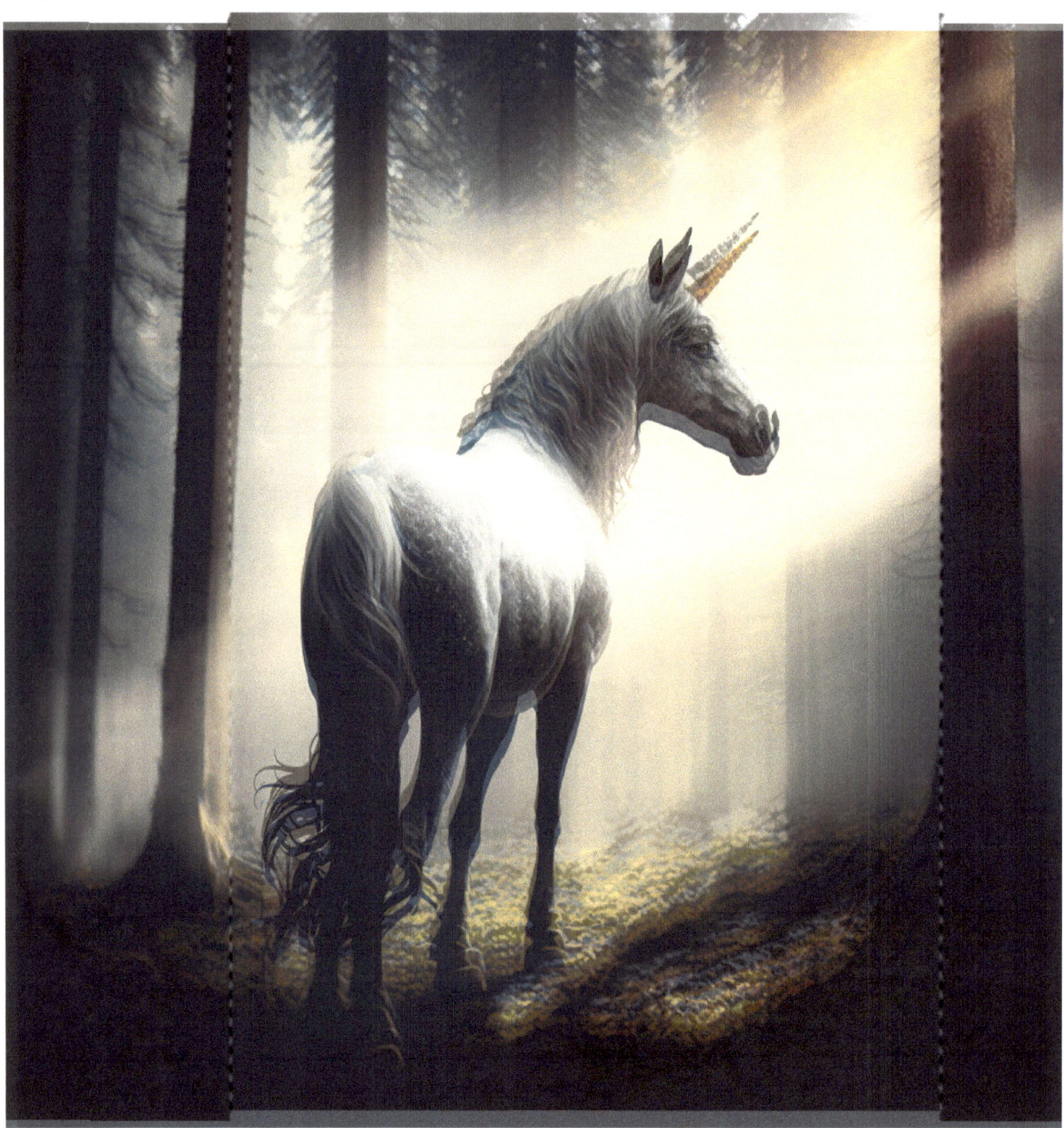

Prompt: Create a scene of a dragon in flight, soaring high above a craggy mountain range, breathing fire and smoke as it roars across the sky.

Output:

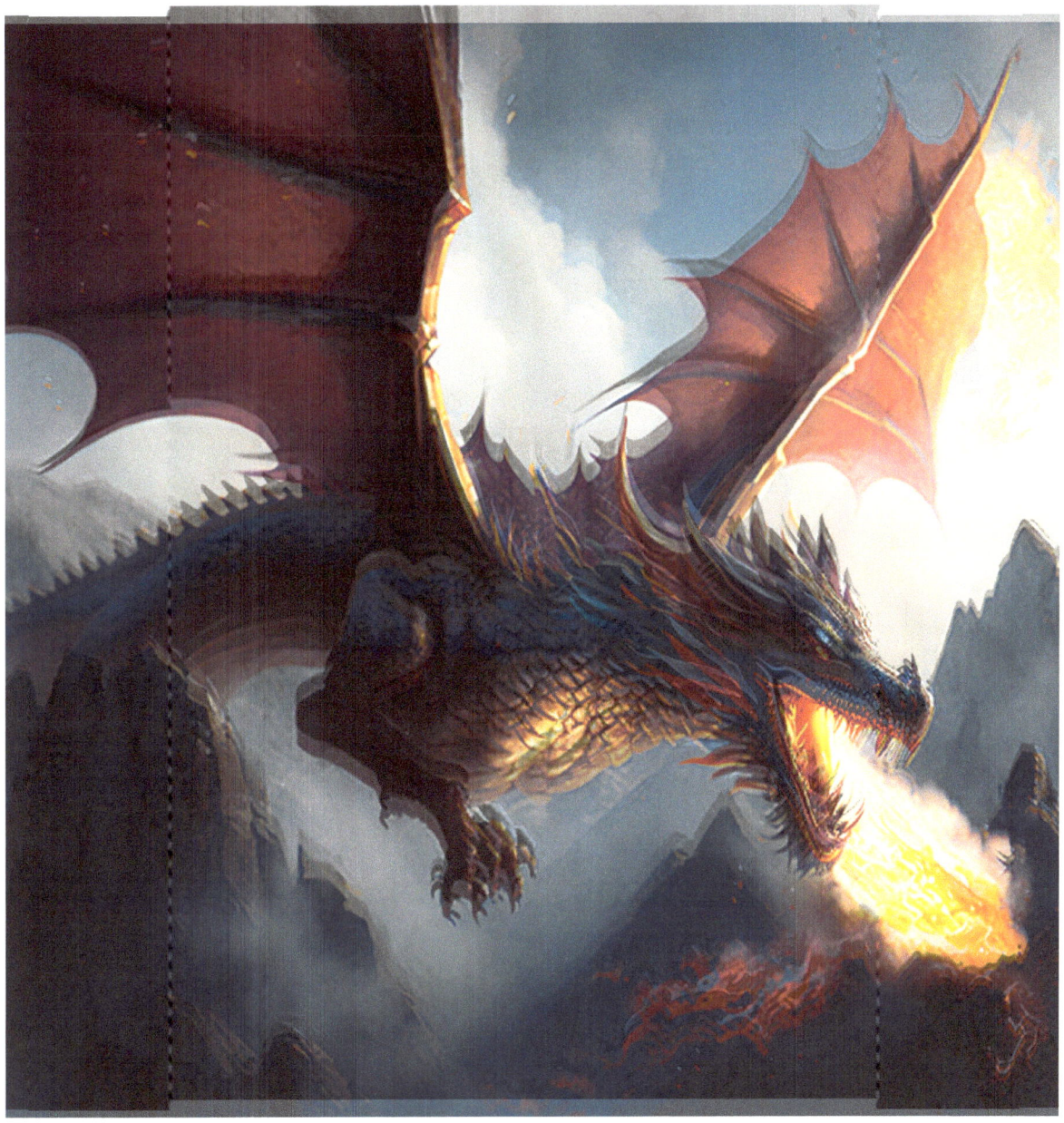

Prompt: Create an image of a ruined city, with crumbling skyscrapers, overgrown streets, and broken bridges, with a red, polluted sky above.

Output:

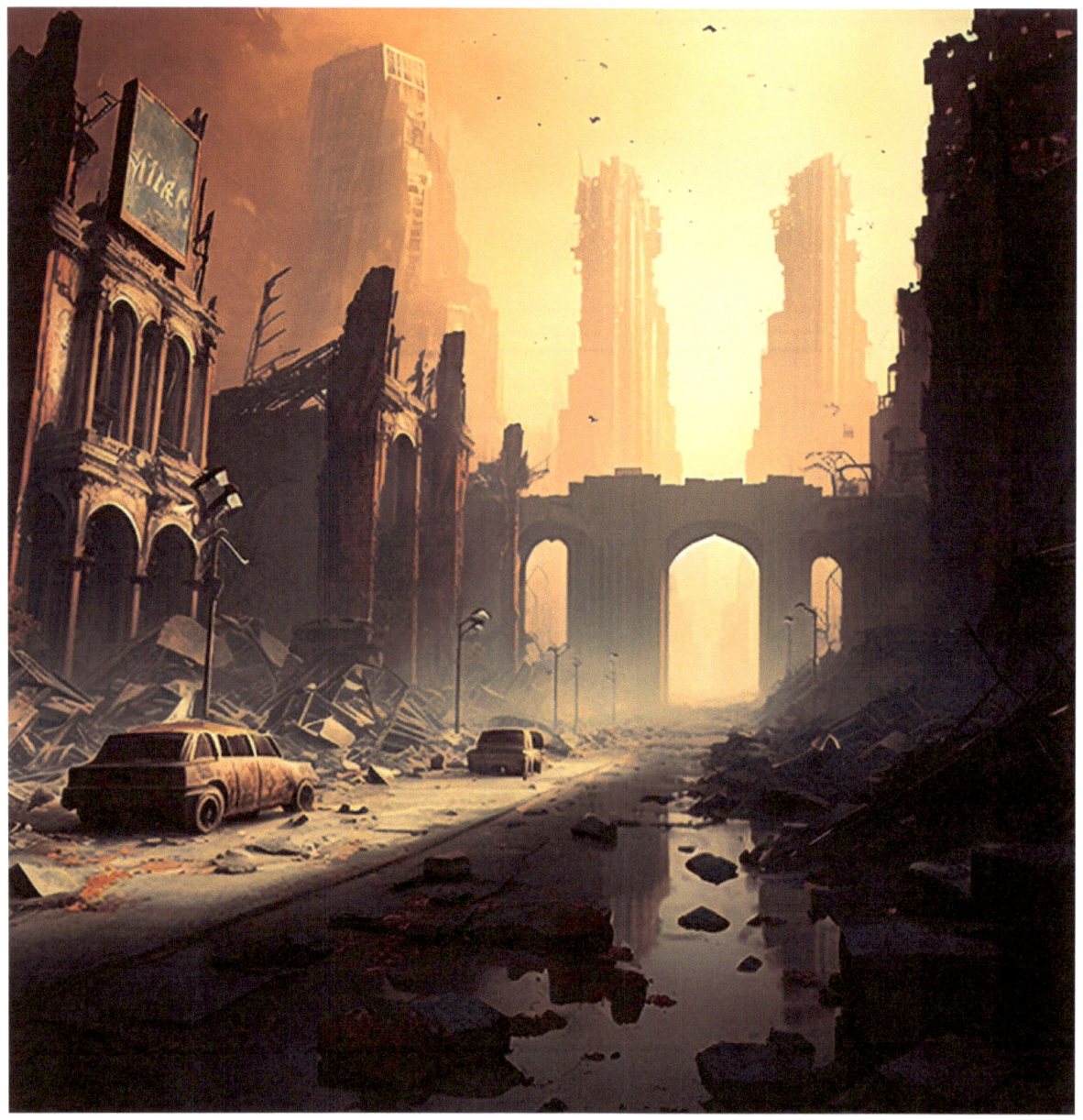

Prompt: Generate a scene of a survivor wandering through a deserted city, with abandoned cars, toppled buildings, and a distant storm approaching.

Output:

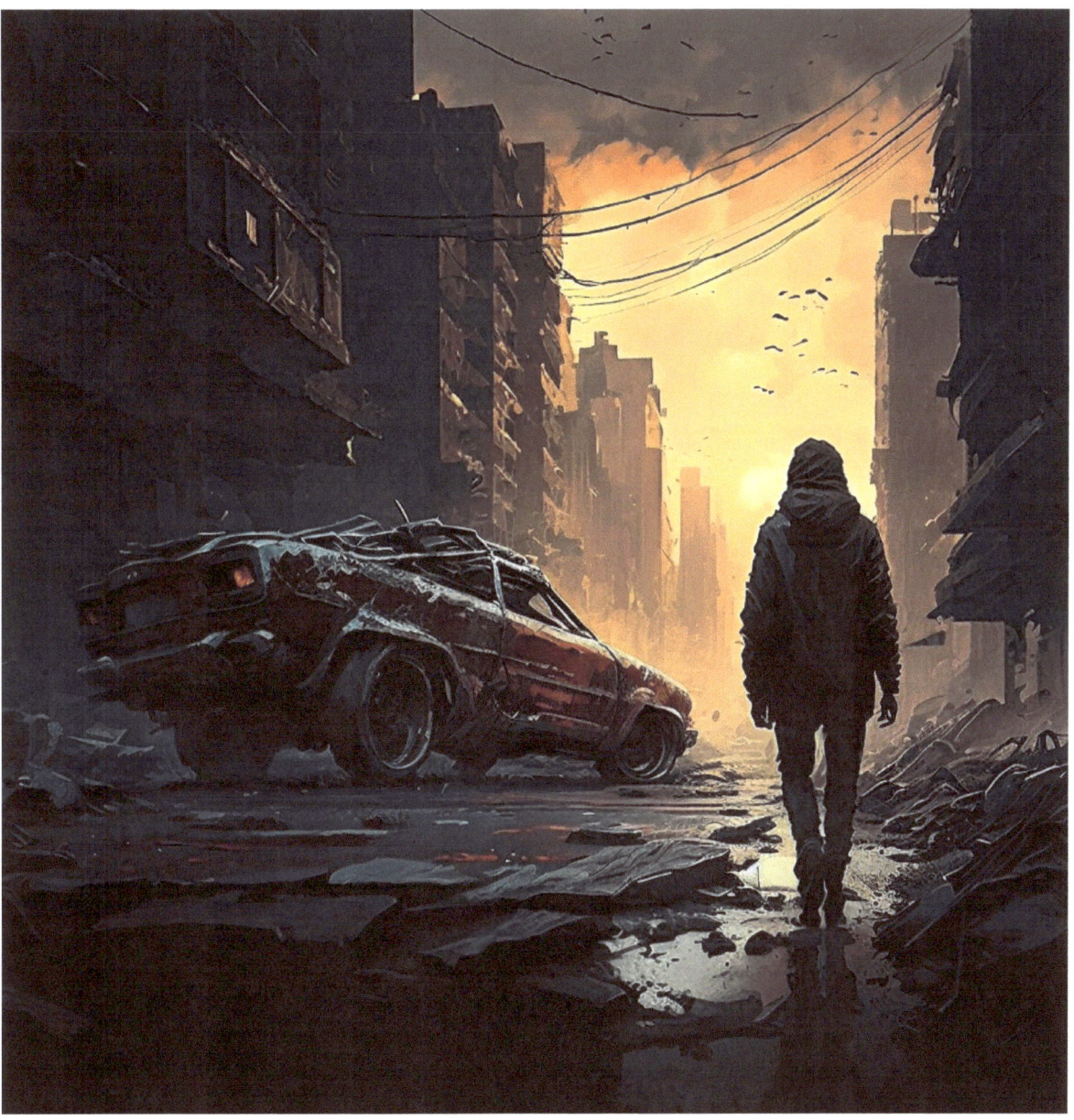

Prompt: Create an image of a towering robot standing guard in a decaying, post-apocalyptic metropolis, with scavengers and bandits lurking in the shadows.

Output:

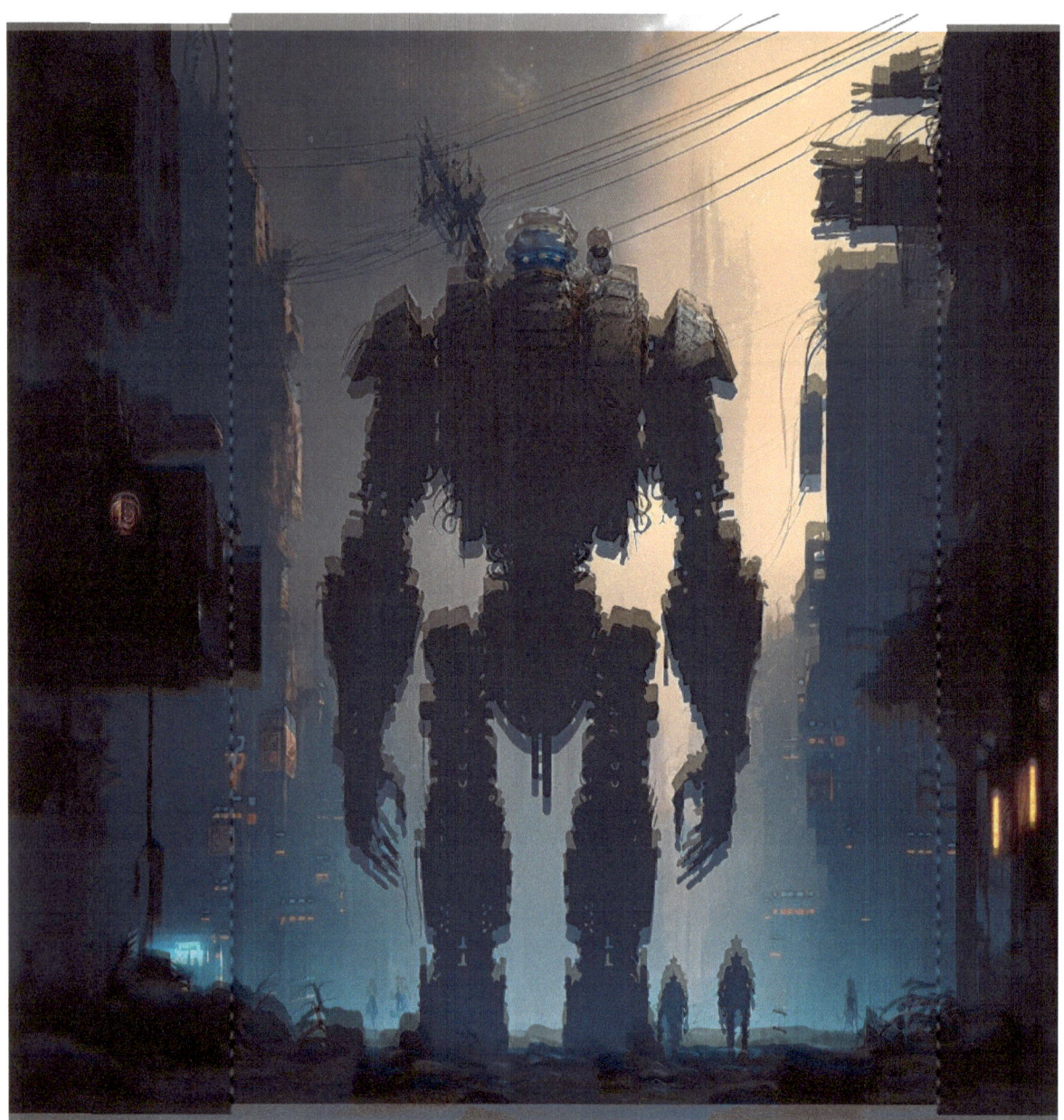

Prompt: Generate a portrait of a lone wanderer standing on a rooftop, looking out over a desolate cityscape with only the sound of wind and distant gunfire.

Output:

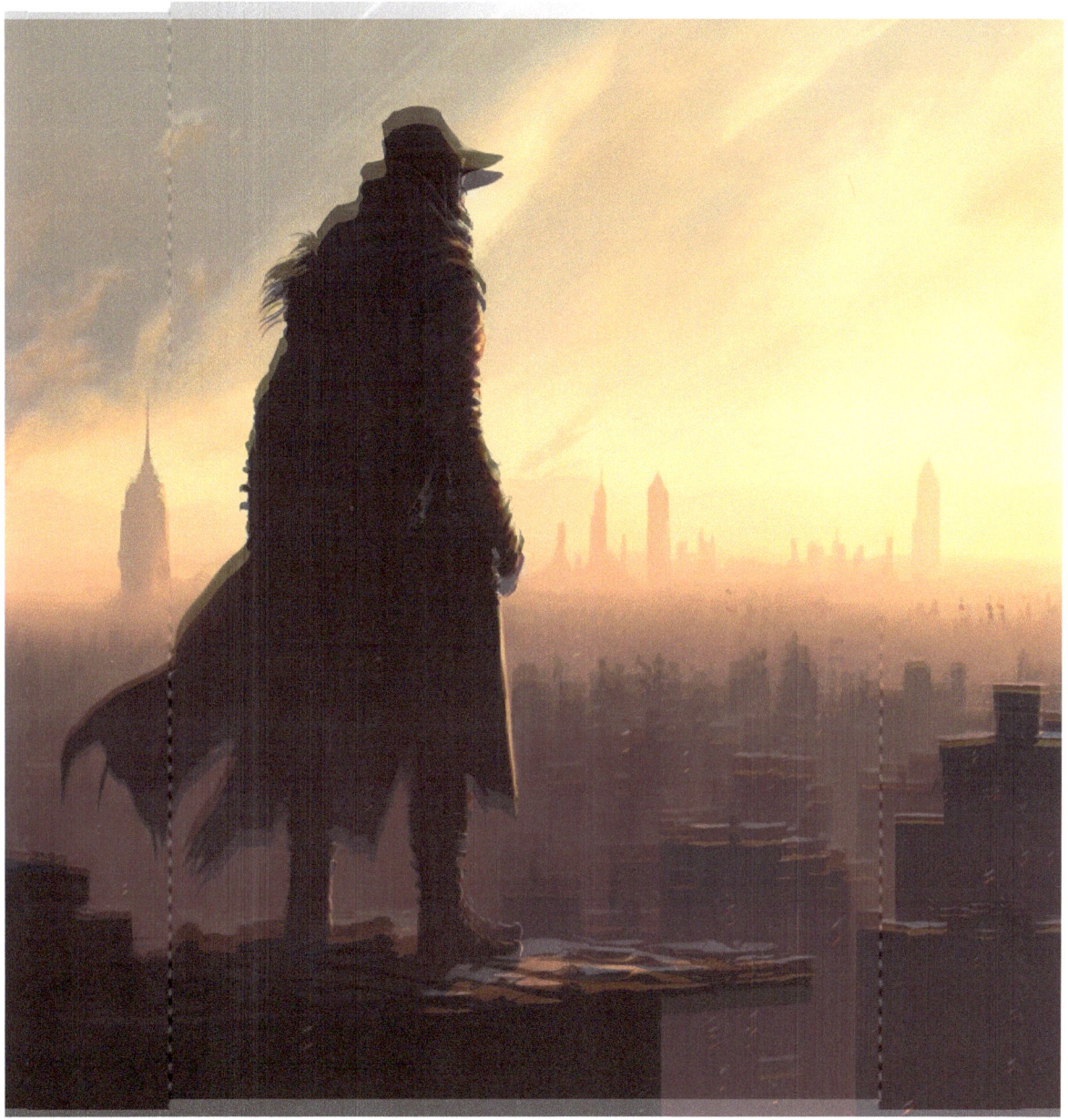

Prompt: Create a scene of a small group of survivors huddled around a campfire in a ruined city, with a ruined skyline in the distance and a feeling of hopelessness and despair.

Output:

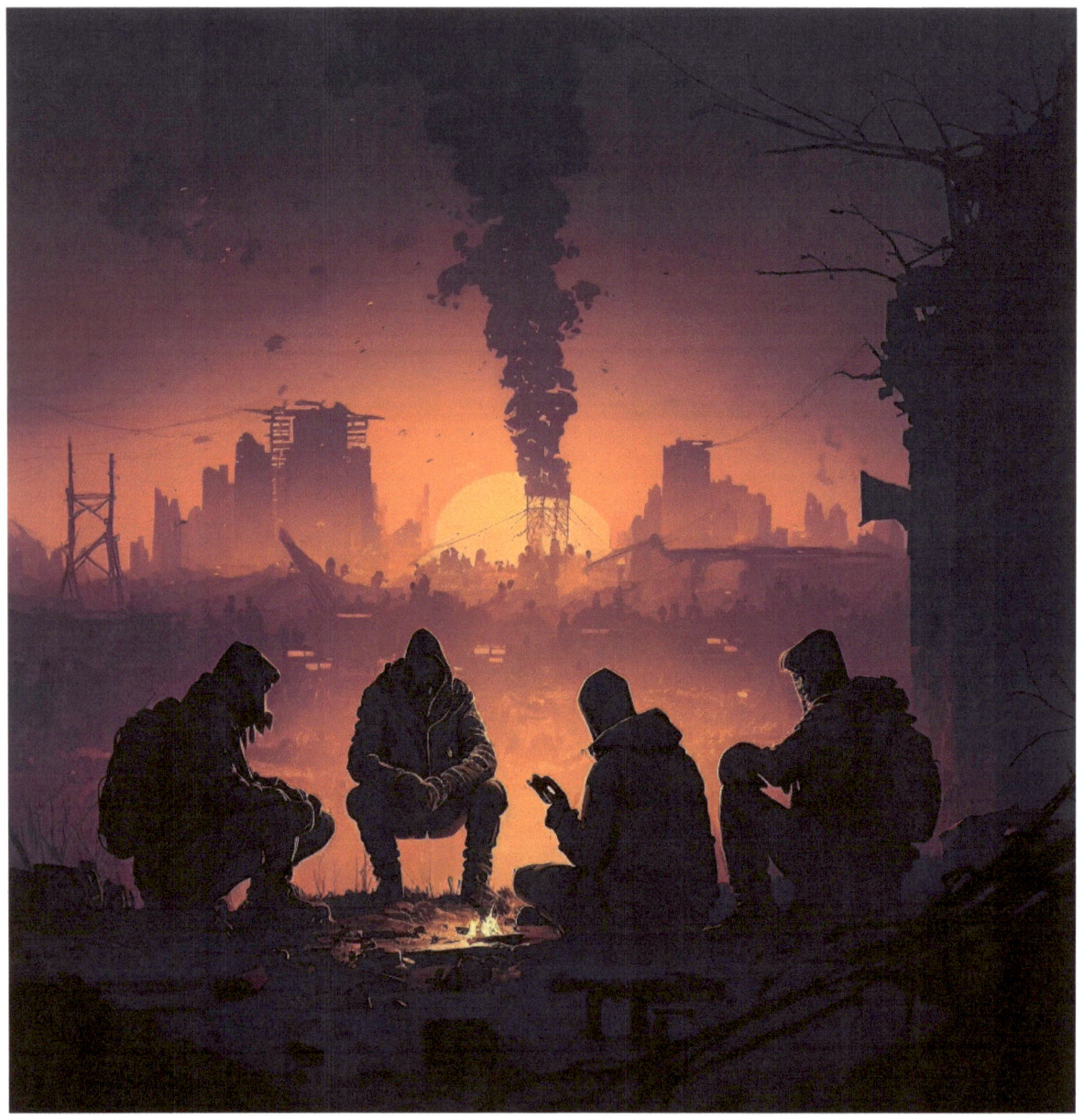

Prompt: Create an image of a gleaming, futuristic city with towering skyscrapers, flying cars, and advanced holographic displays.

Output:

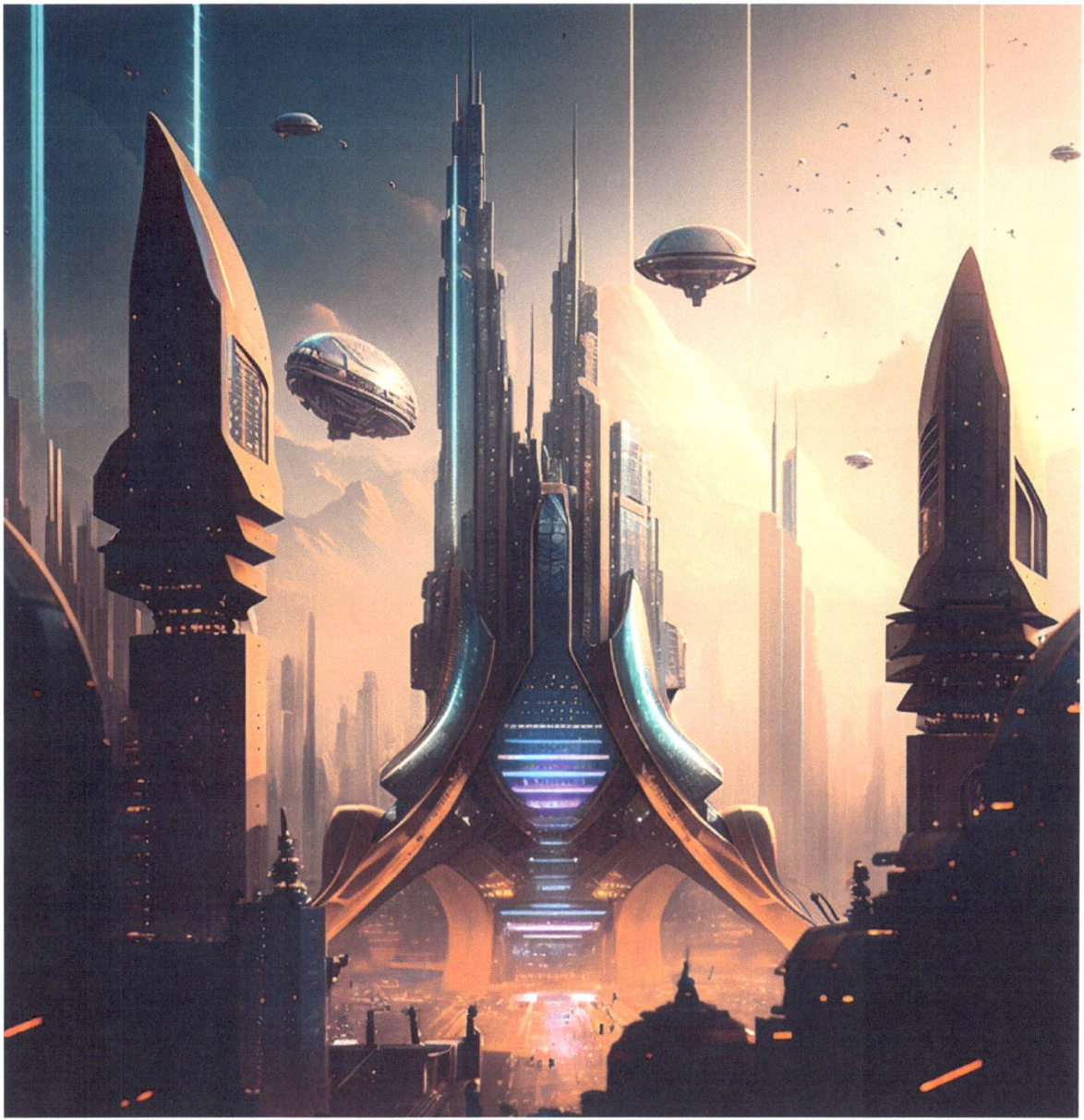

Prompt: Create an image of a massive space station orbiting a distant planet, with sleek, streamlined ships docked at its ports and a ring of light surrounding the station.

Output:

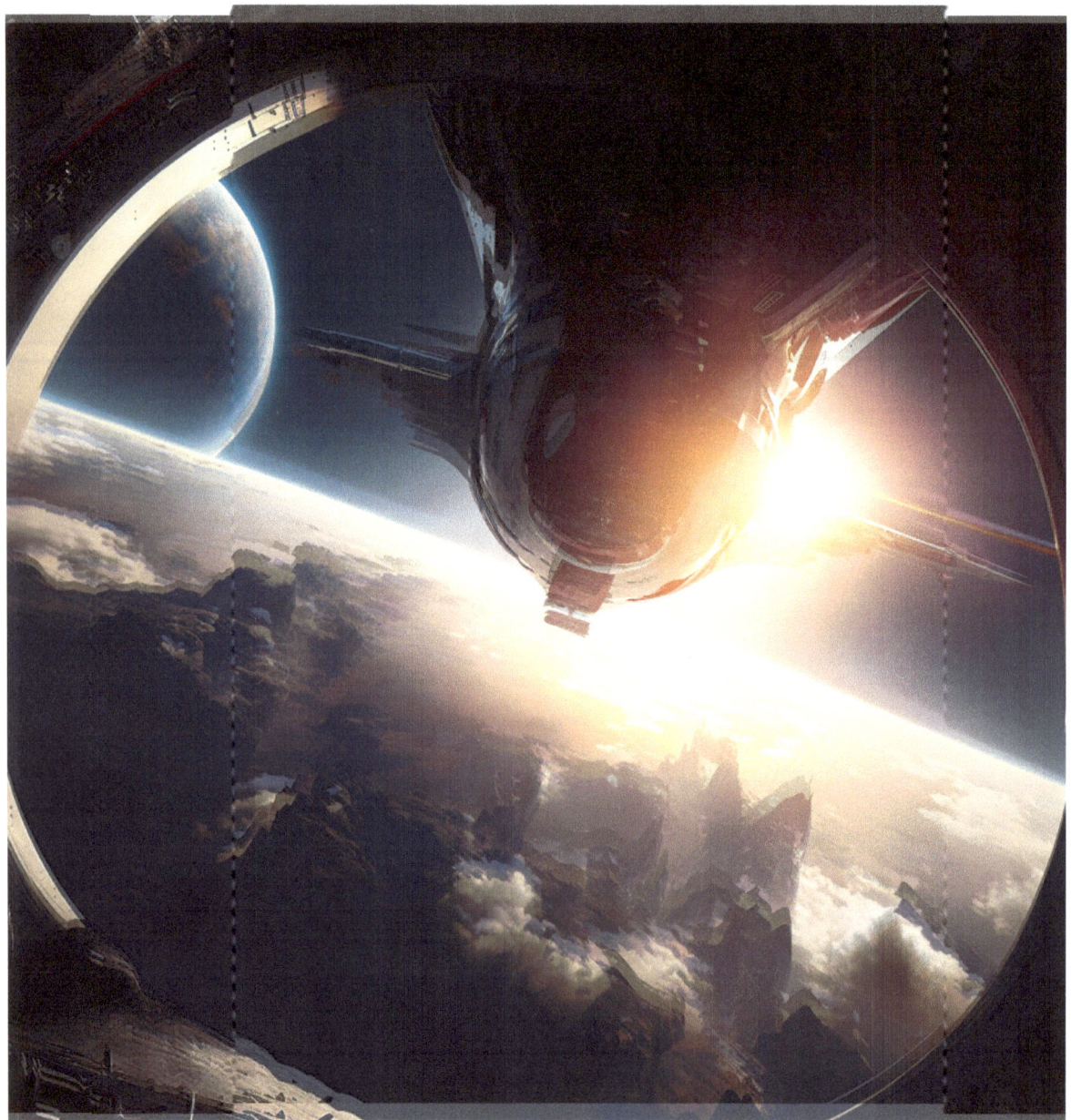

Prompt: Generate a scene of a team of explorers exploring a strange, alien landscape, with towering rock formations and glowing flora.

Output:

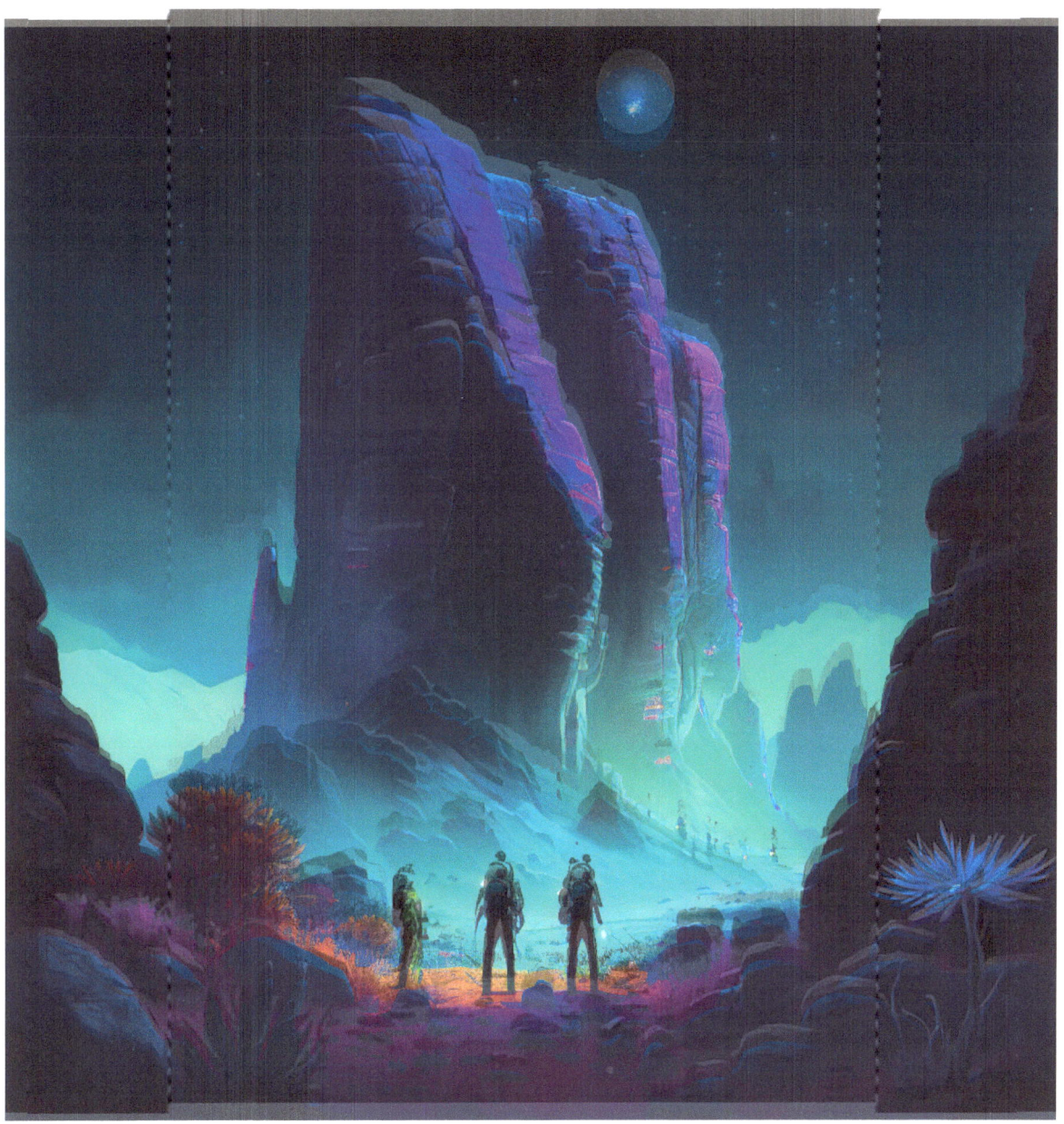

Prompt: Create an image of a sprawling, intergalactic trade hub, with creatures from dozens of different planets haggling over exotic goods.

Output:

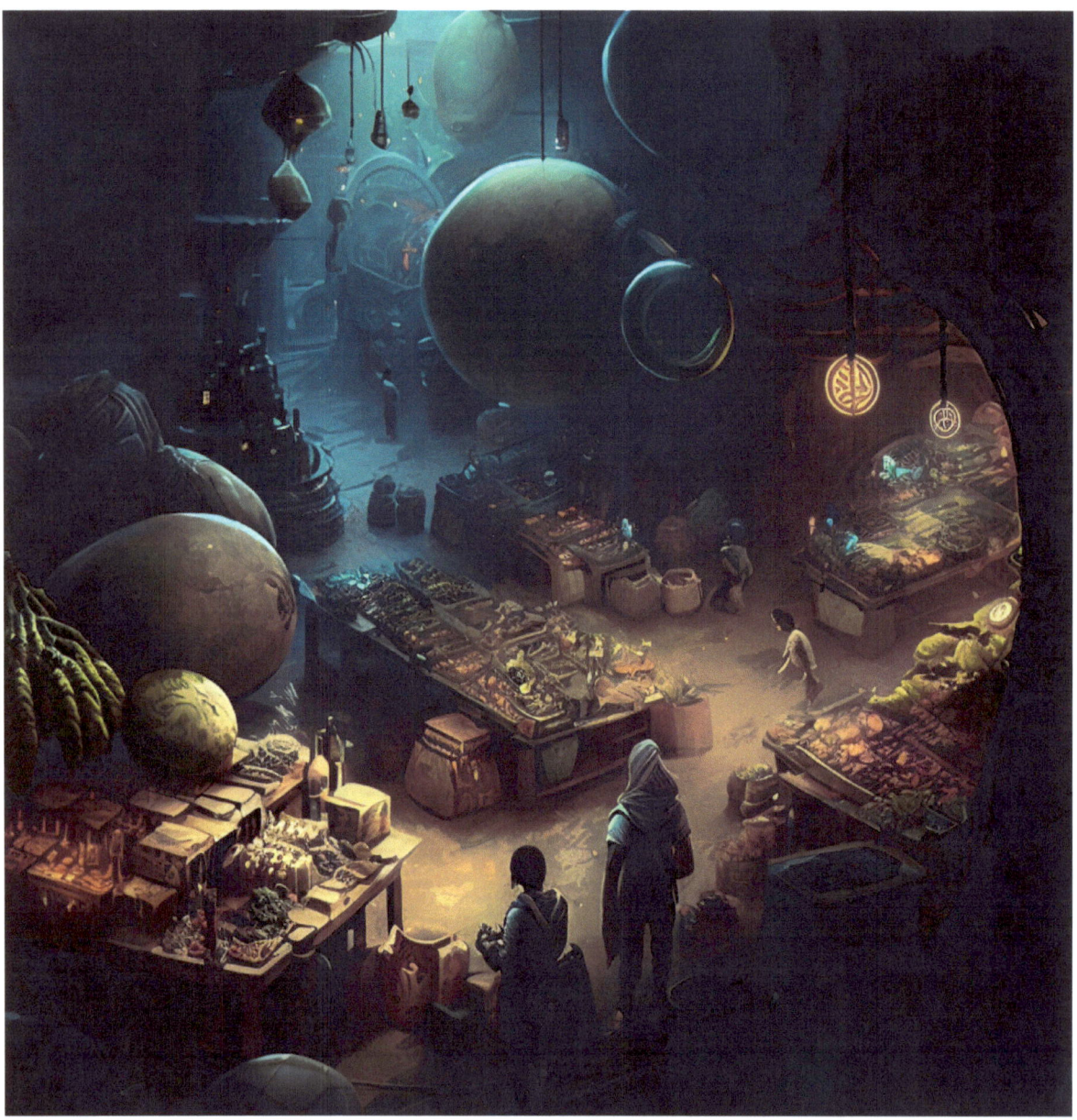

Prompt: Create an image of a cybernetically-enhanced woman standing on a neon-lit street corner in a bustling metropolis, with towering buildings and flying cars in the background.

Output:

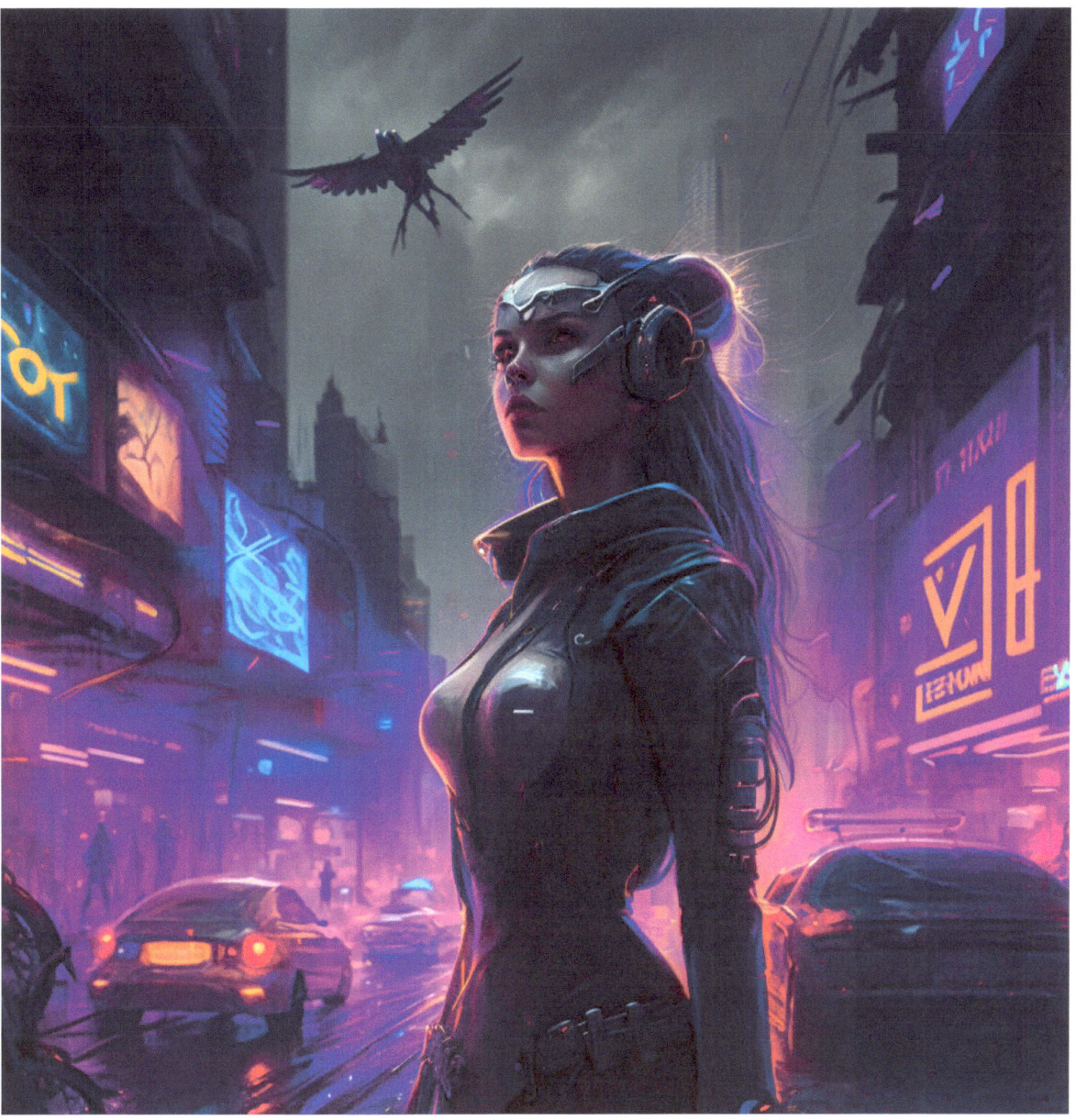

Prompt: Generate a scene of a bounty hunter in a dark, rain-soaked alley, with glowing cybernetic implants and a futuristic gun at the ready.

Output:

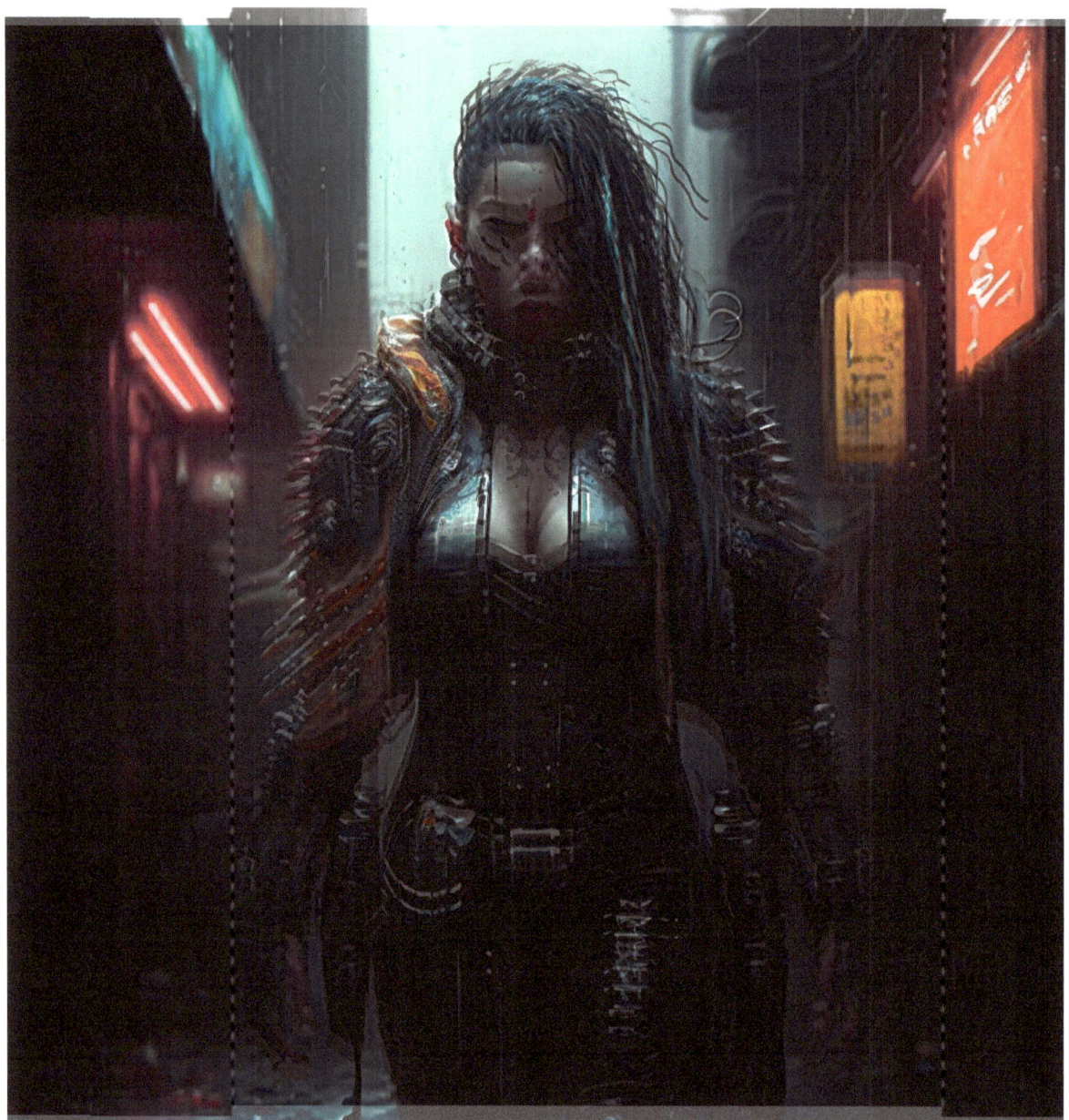

Prompt: Create an image of a cyberpunk nightclub, with holographic dancers and patrons in a variety of cyberpunk fashions, surrounded by flashing neon lights and towering skyscrapers.

Output:

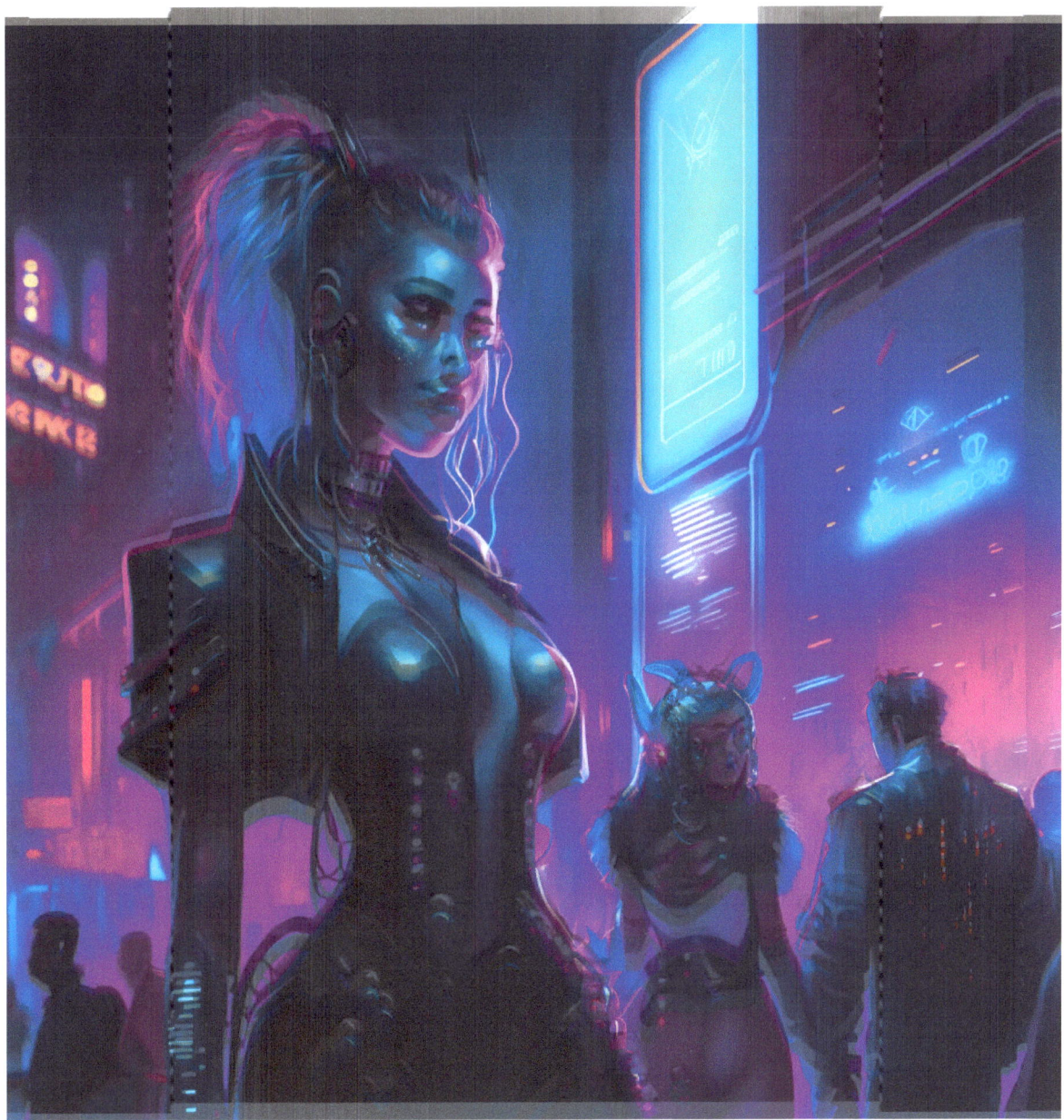

Prompt: Generate a portrait of a hacker wearing a hooded cloak, illuminated by the glow of a computer screen, surrounded by various cybernetic implants and gadgets.

Output:

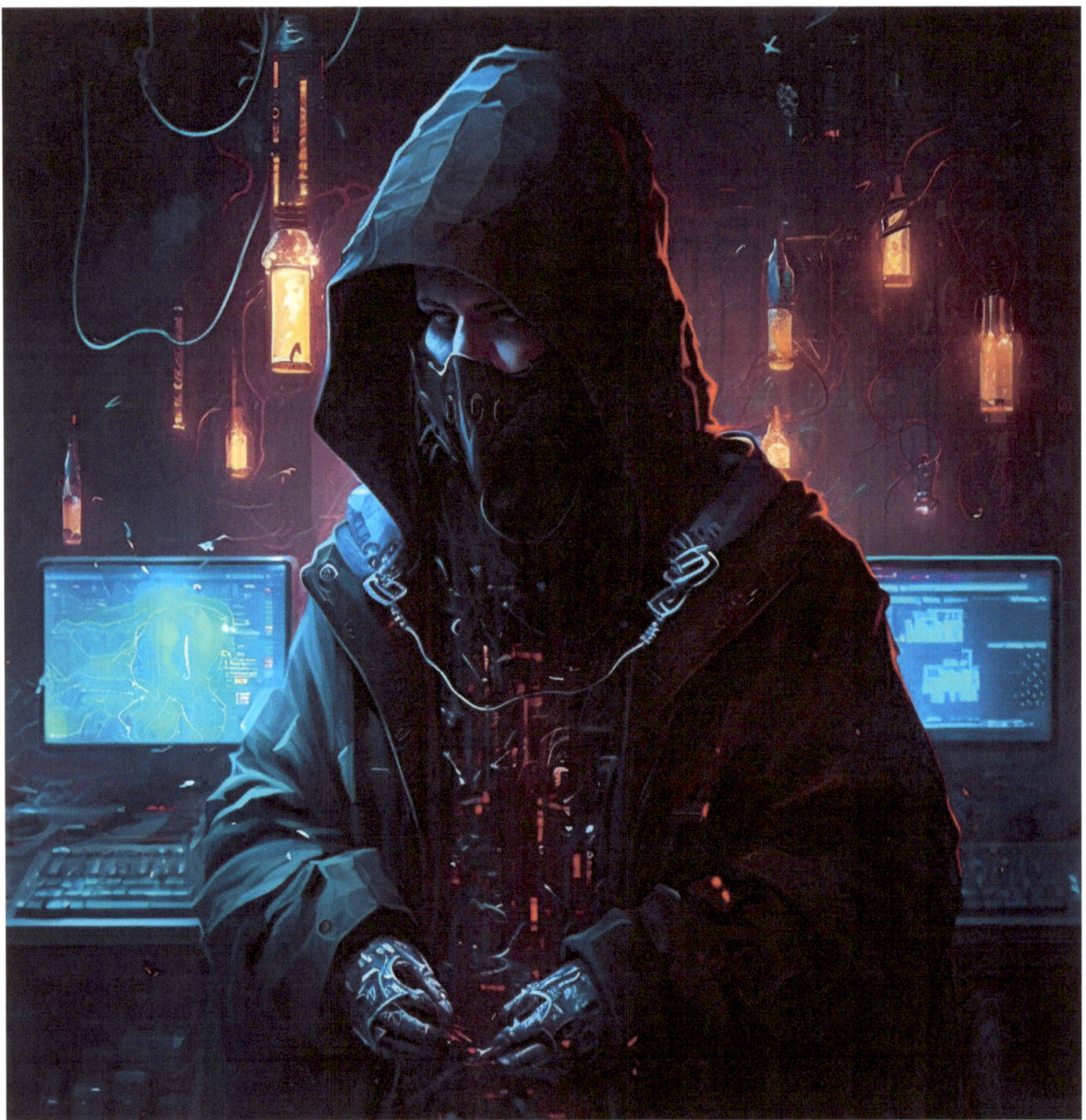

Prompt: Create an image of a futuristic market, with vendors selling exotic cybernetic implants and other cyberpunk wares under a massive holographic advertising sign.

Output:

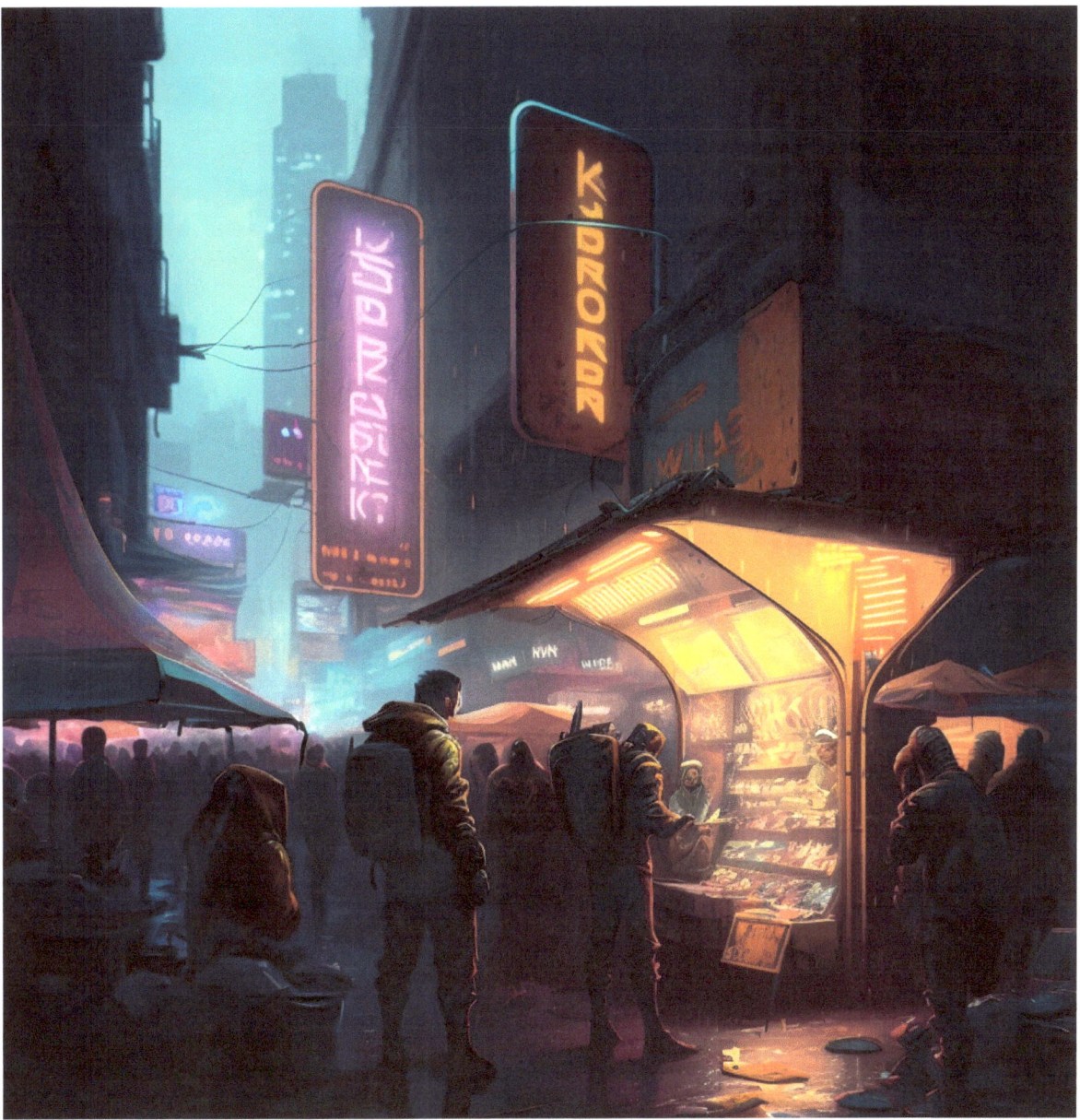

7 PROMPT ENGINEERING

Welcome to the section where we showcase some examples of the various types of prompts which you can utilize when generating your images. The following pages are filled with exciting, beautiful, and sometimes unexpected images generated by AI algorithms based on different types of prompts.

From object-specific prompts that generate images of specific objects or animals, to mood-specific prompts that create images with a particular feeling or atmosphere, each example demonstrates the power and versatility of AI-generated art.

We have also included examples of style-specific prompts that generate images in a specific artistic style or based on a particular artist's works. And for those who are feeling adventurous, we have some examples of randomized prompts that produce unpredictable and fascinating images.

We hope that these examples will inspire you to experiment with different prompts and explore the possibilities of AI-generated art. With the right prompt and algorithm, you never know what kind of art you might create. So, let's dive in and see what the power of AI can do!

Object-specific prompts

Prompt: Generate a realistic image of a red Ferrari sports car in motion, with a blurred background.

Output:

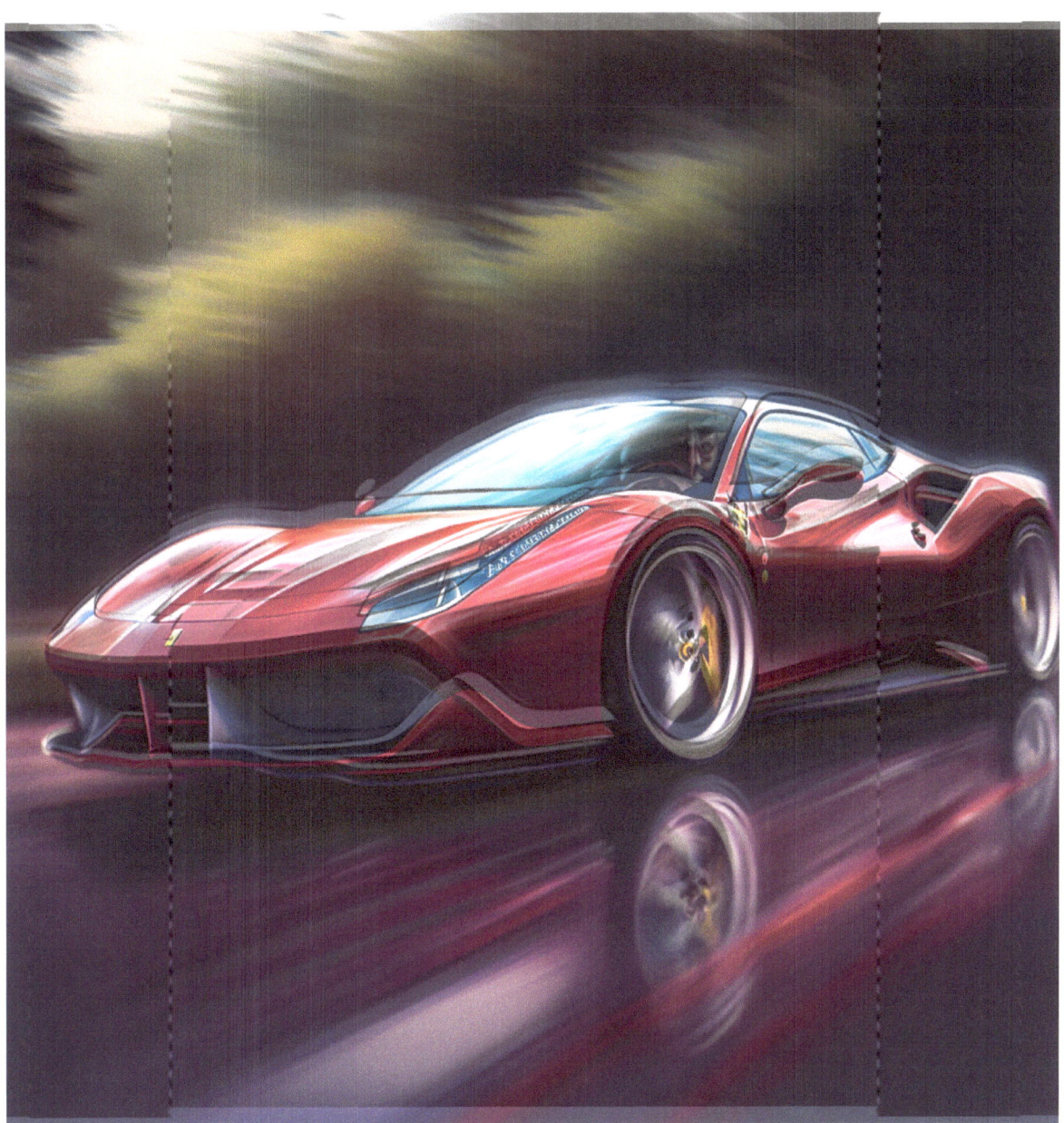

Prompt: Create an abstract image of a bird in flight, with vibrant colours and sharp lines..

Output:

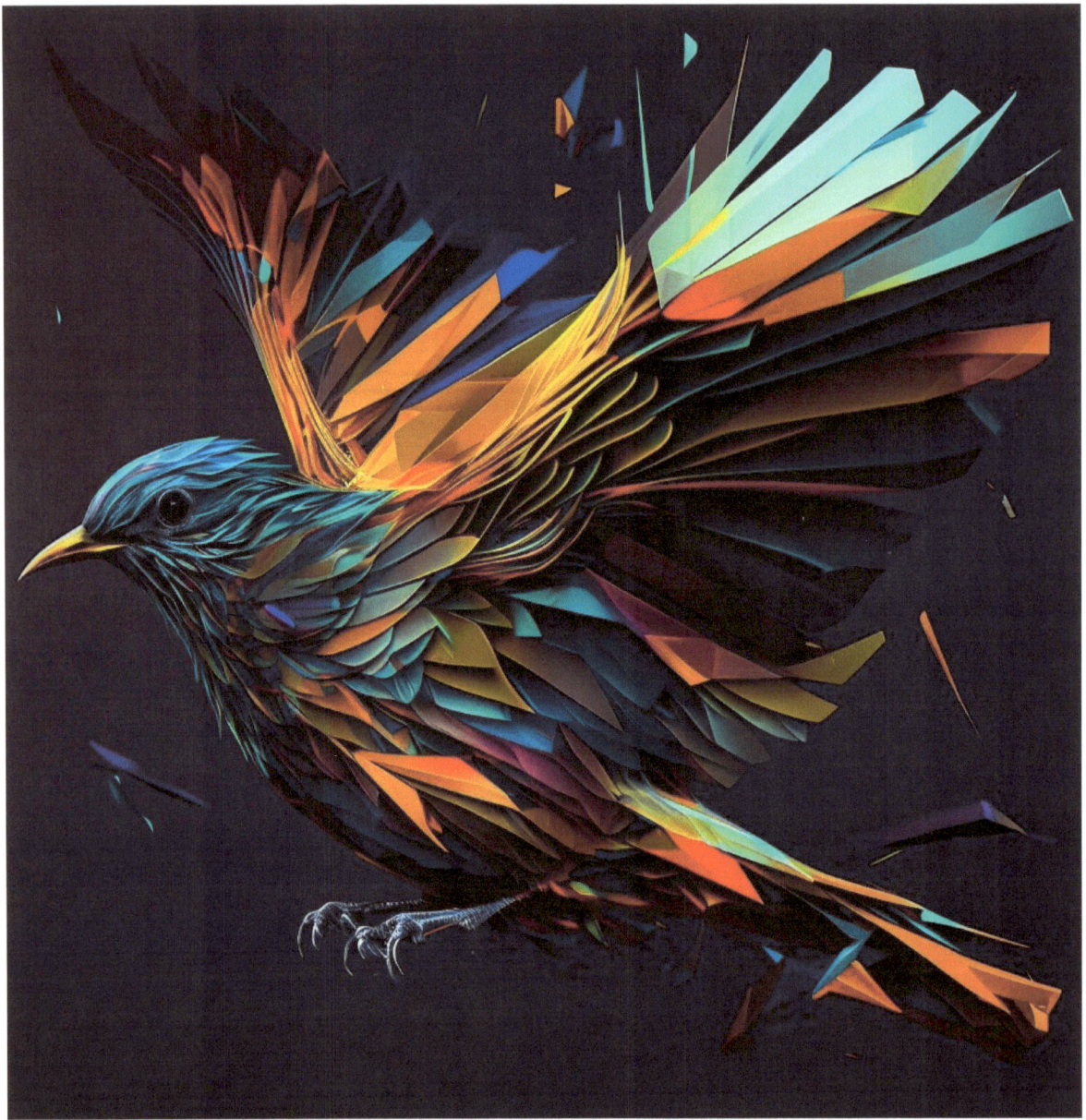

Prompt: Create a surrealist image of a colorful fish swimming through the clouds.

Output:

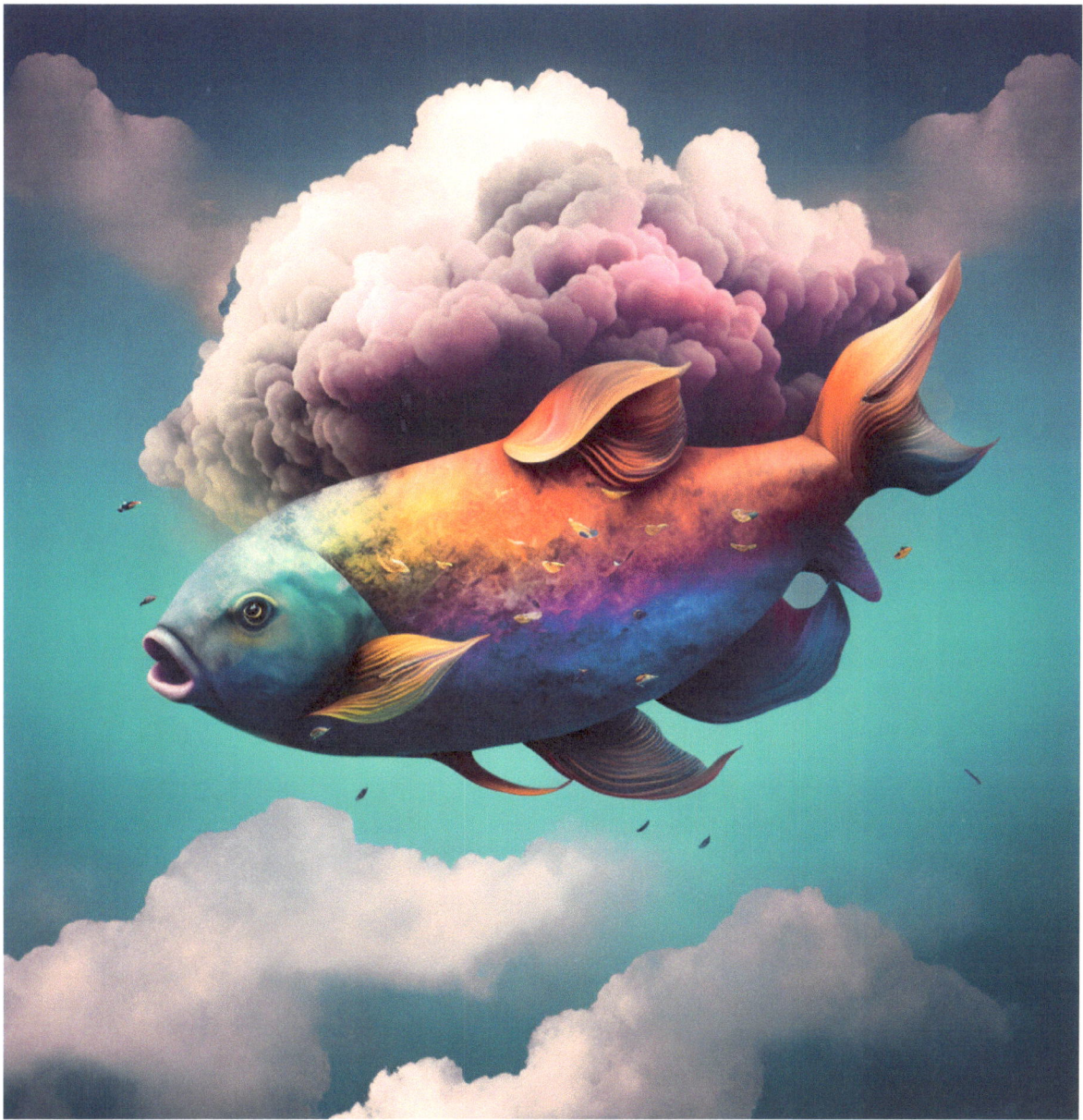

Style-specific prompts

Prompt: Create an image in the style of Van Gogh's 'Starry Night', but with a cityscape instead of a rural scene:

Output:

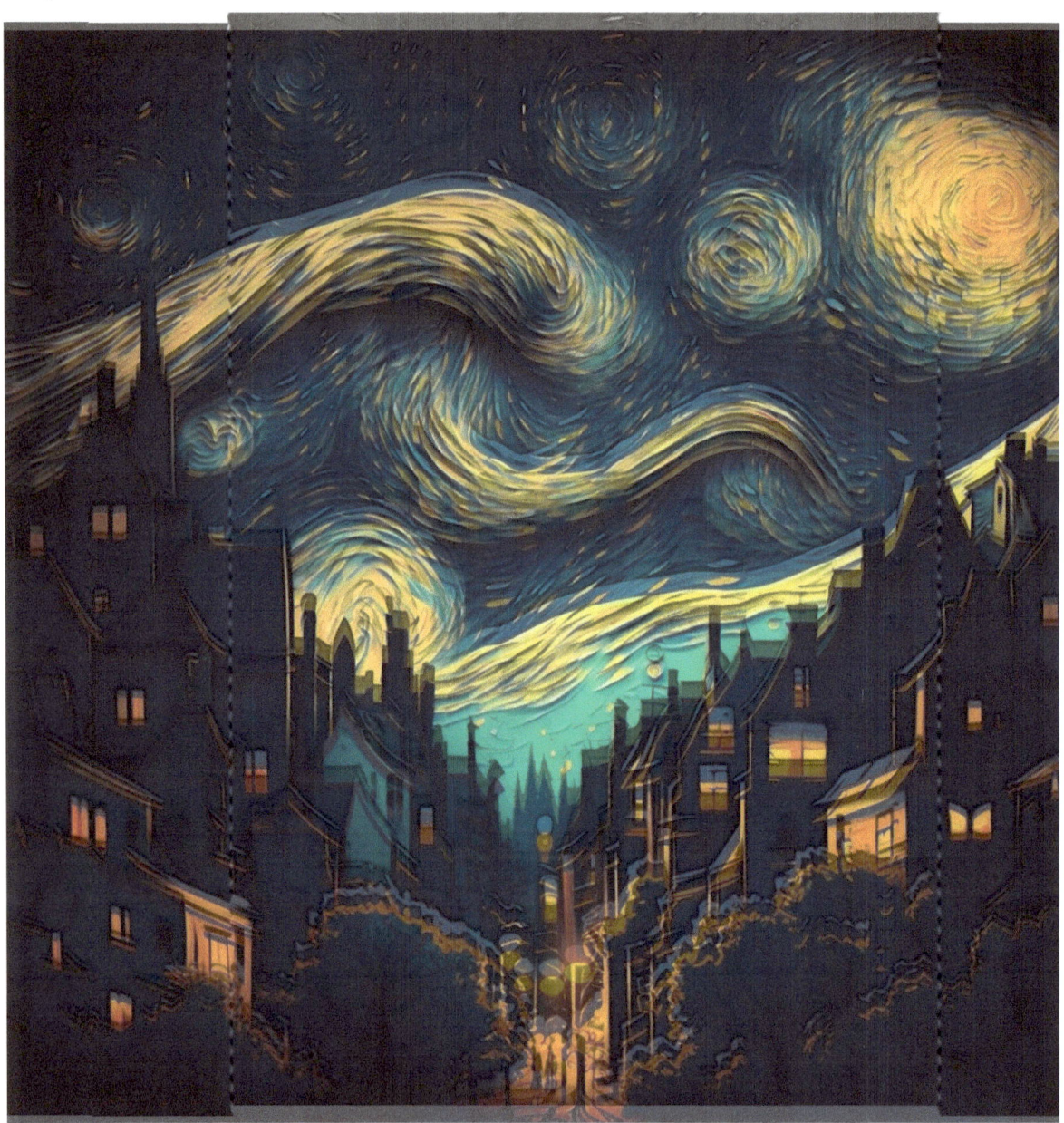

Prompt: Generate an abstract painting in the style of Wassily Kandinsky, using warm colours and geometric shapes.

Output:

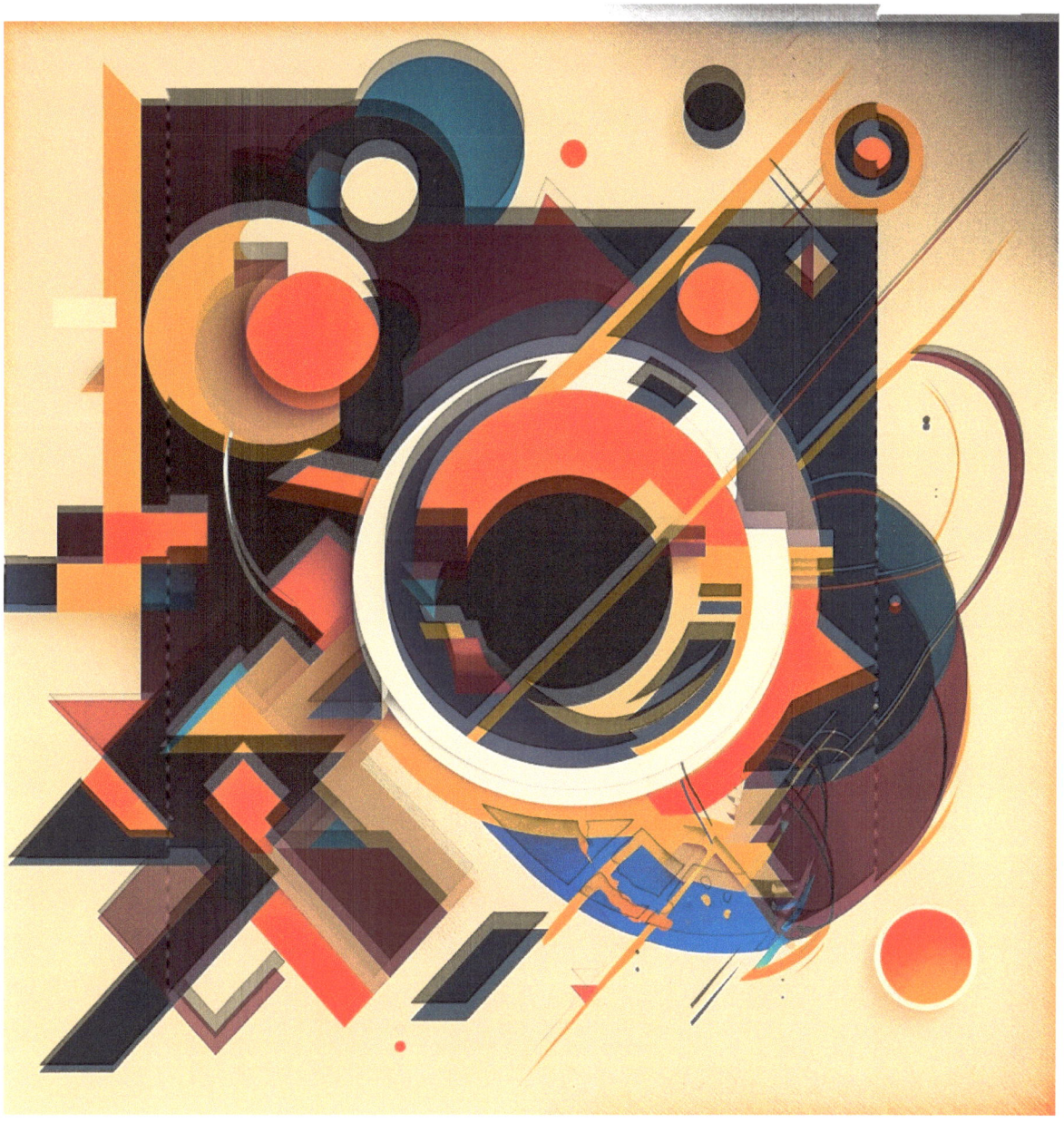

Prompt: Produce a portrait in the style of Rembrandt, using dark lighting and dramatic shadows.

Output:

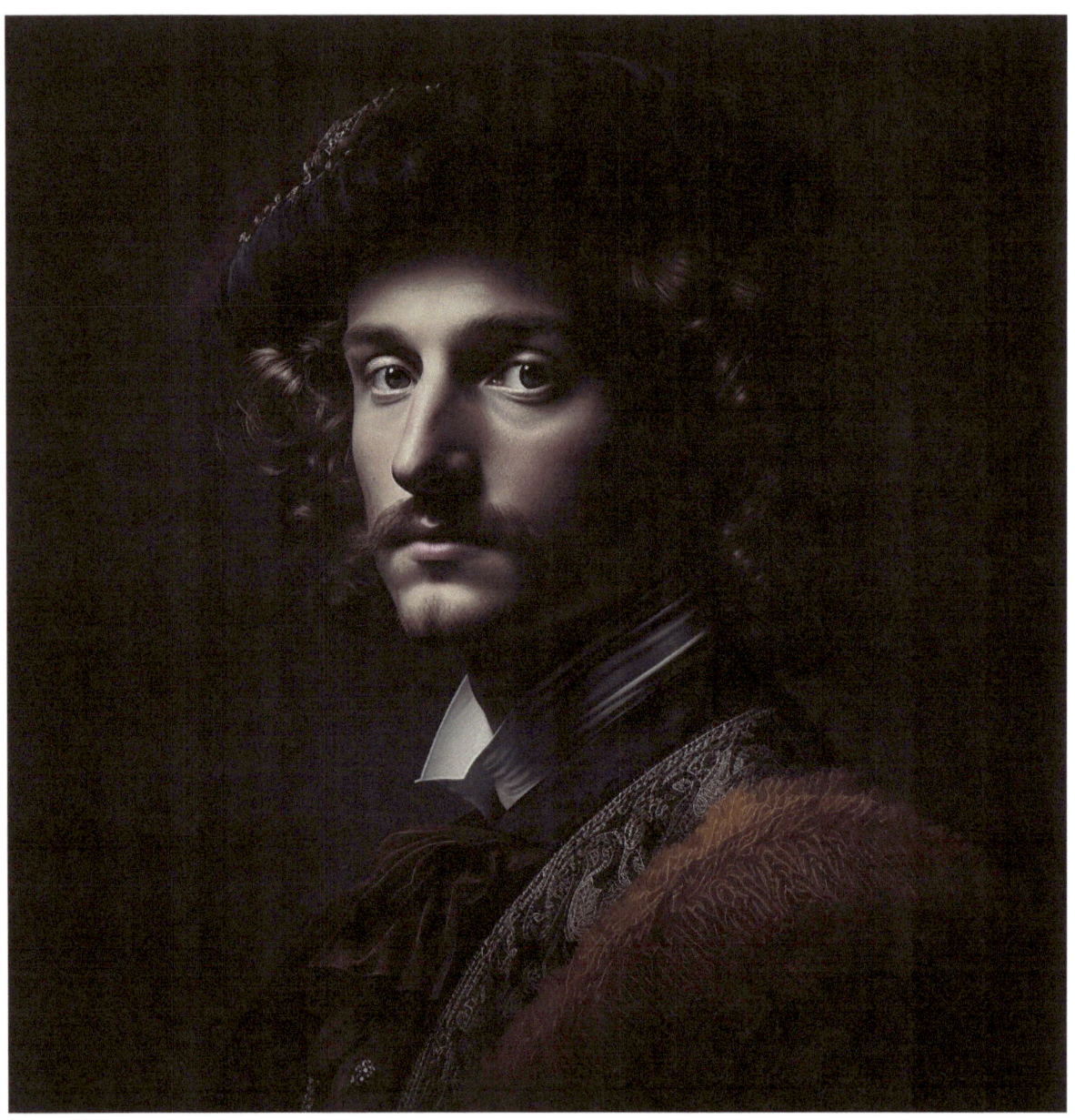

Colour-specific prompts

Prompt: Create an image using shades of blue, inspired by the ocean.

Output:

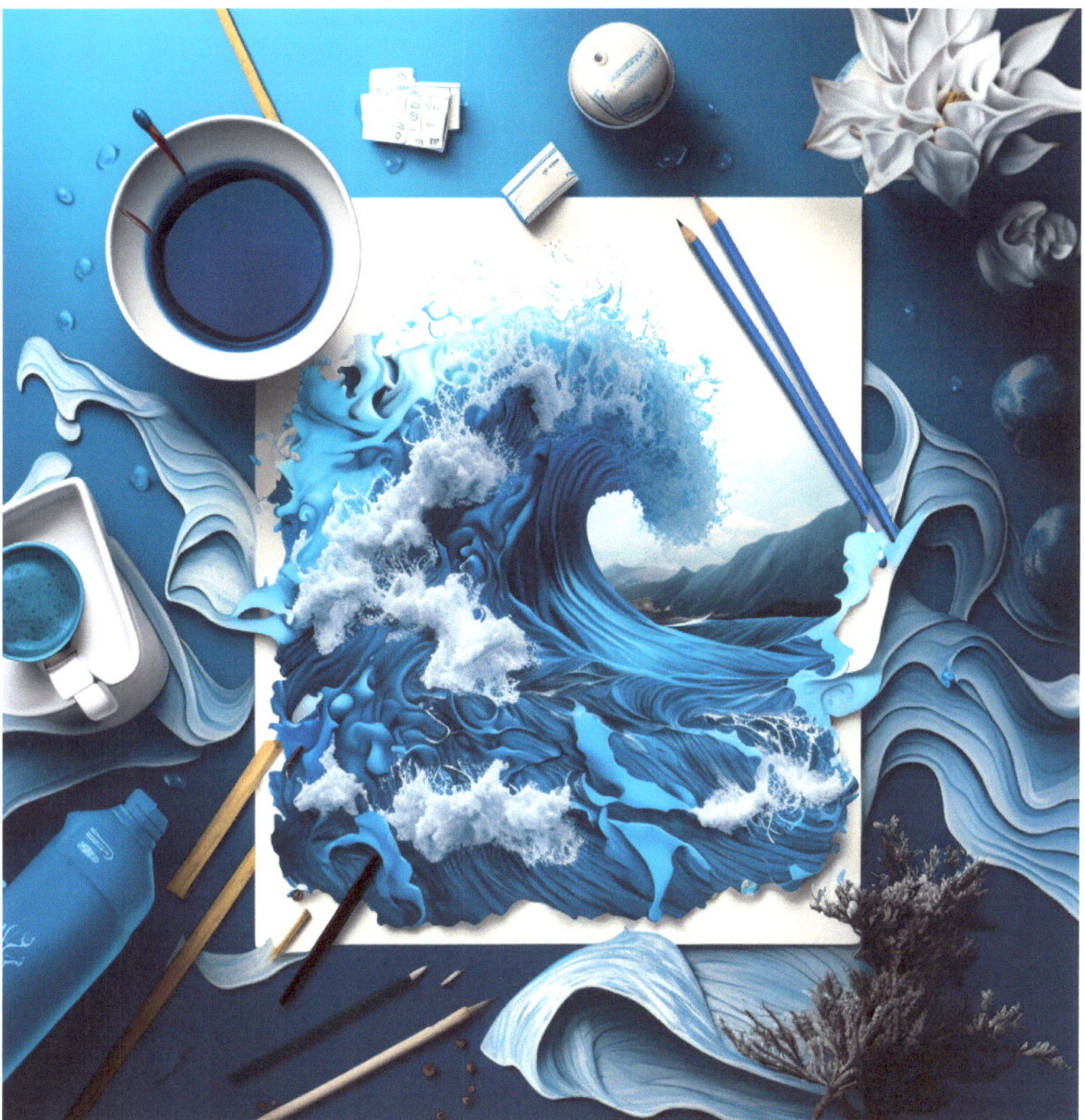

Prompt: Generate an image using shades of red and orange, inspired by a sunset over the desert

Output:

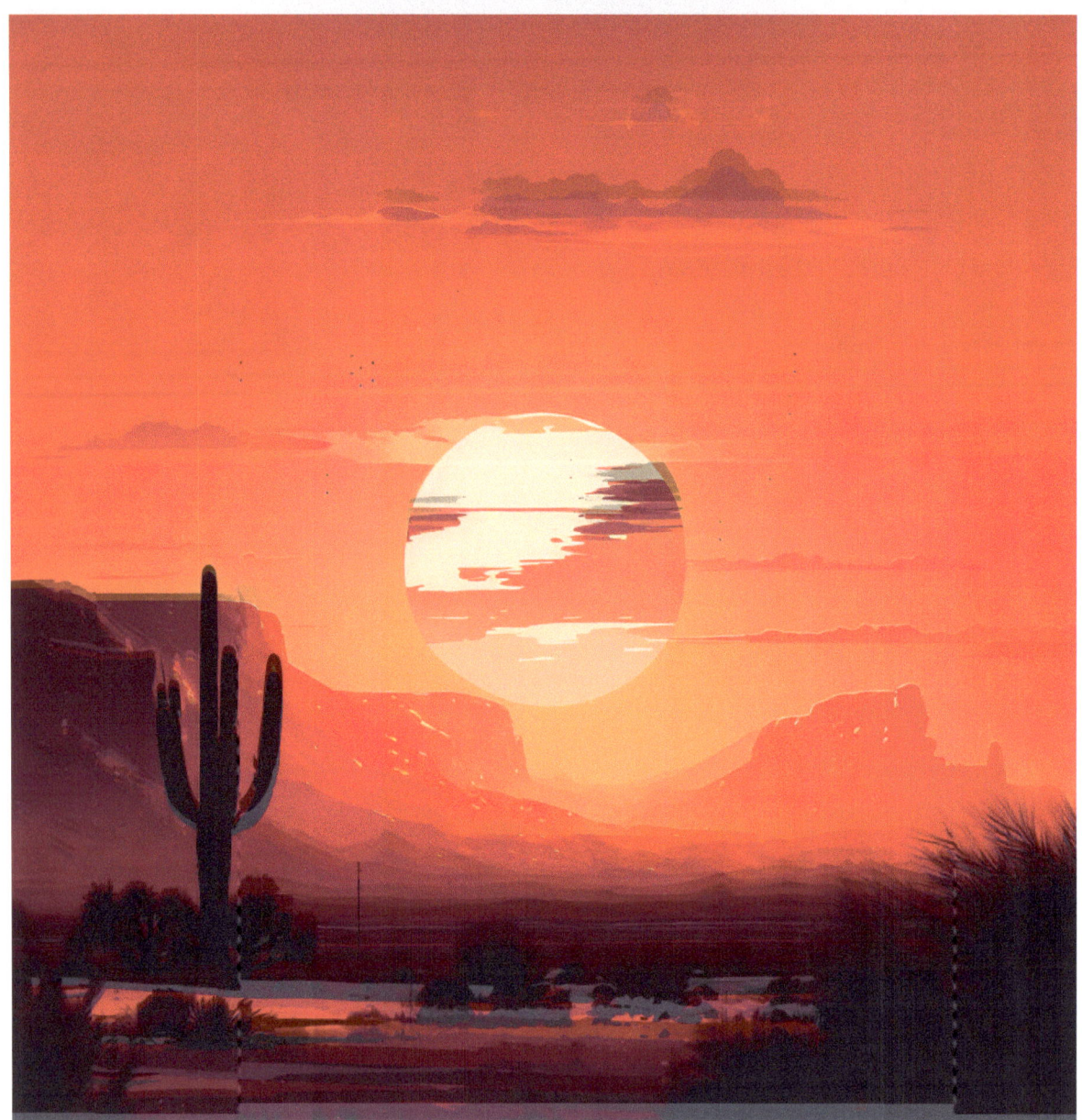

Prompt: Produce an image using contrasting shades of black and neon green.

Output:

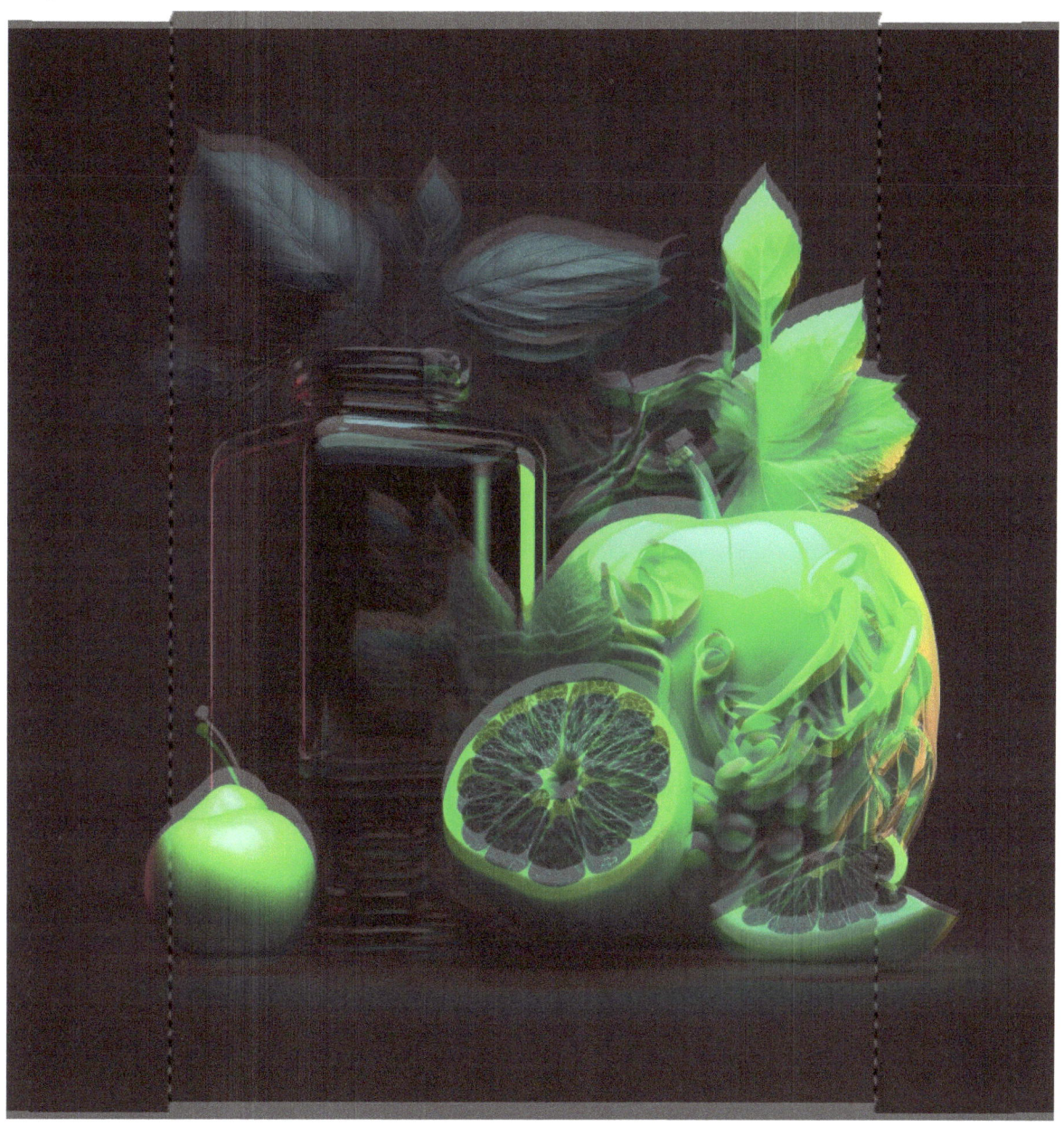

Mood-specific prompts

Prompt: Create an image that evokes a sense of tranquility and calmness.

Output:

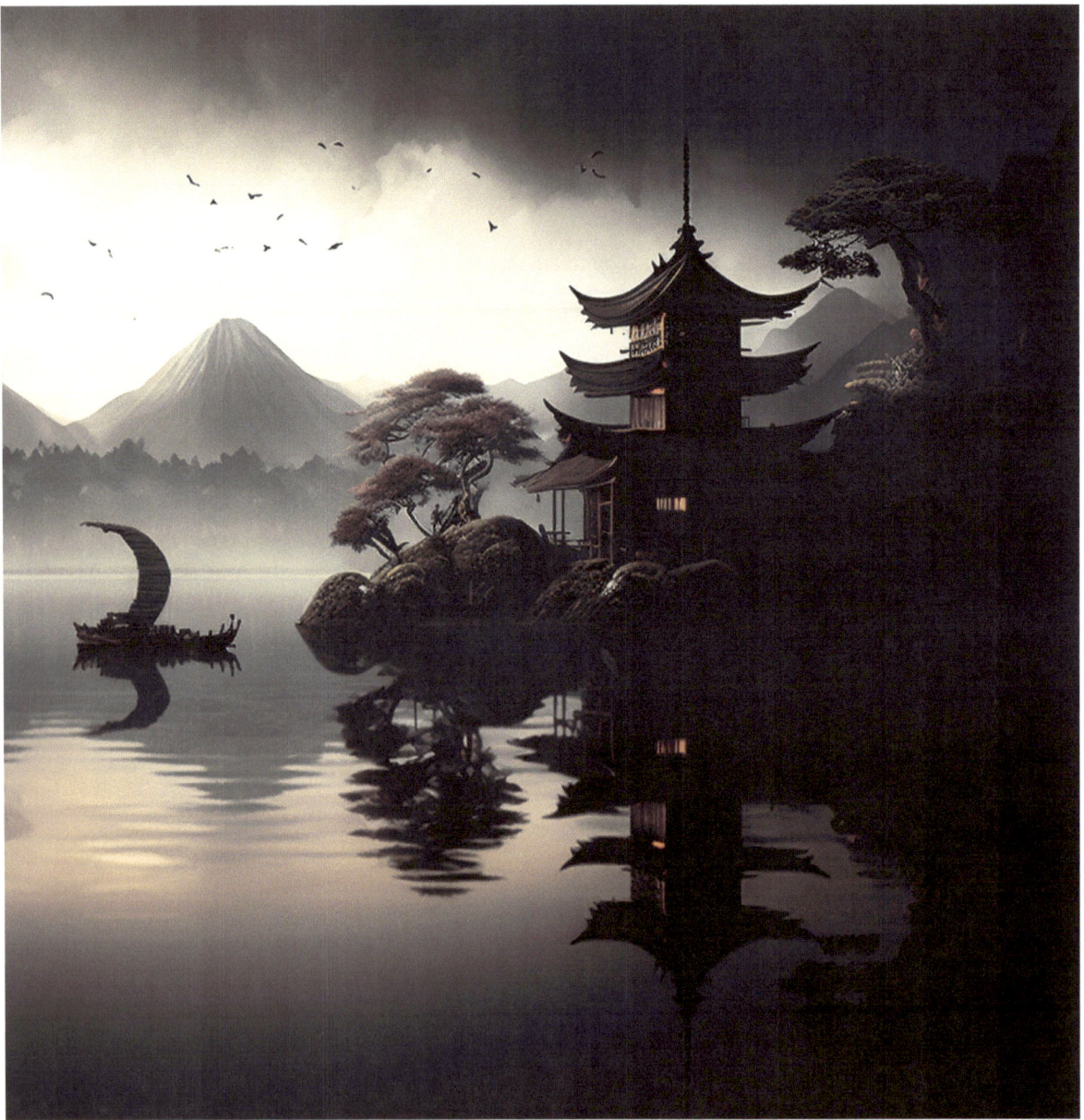

The Beauty of Algorithms: A Collection of AI-Generated Art

Prompt: Generate an artwork that captures the feeling of nostalgia.

Output:

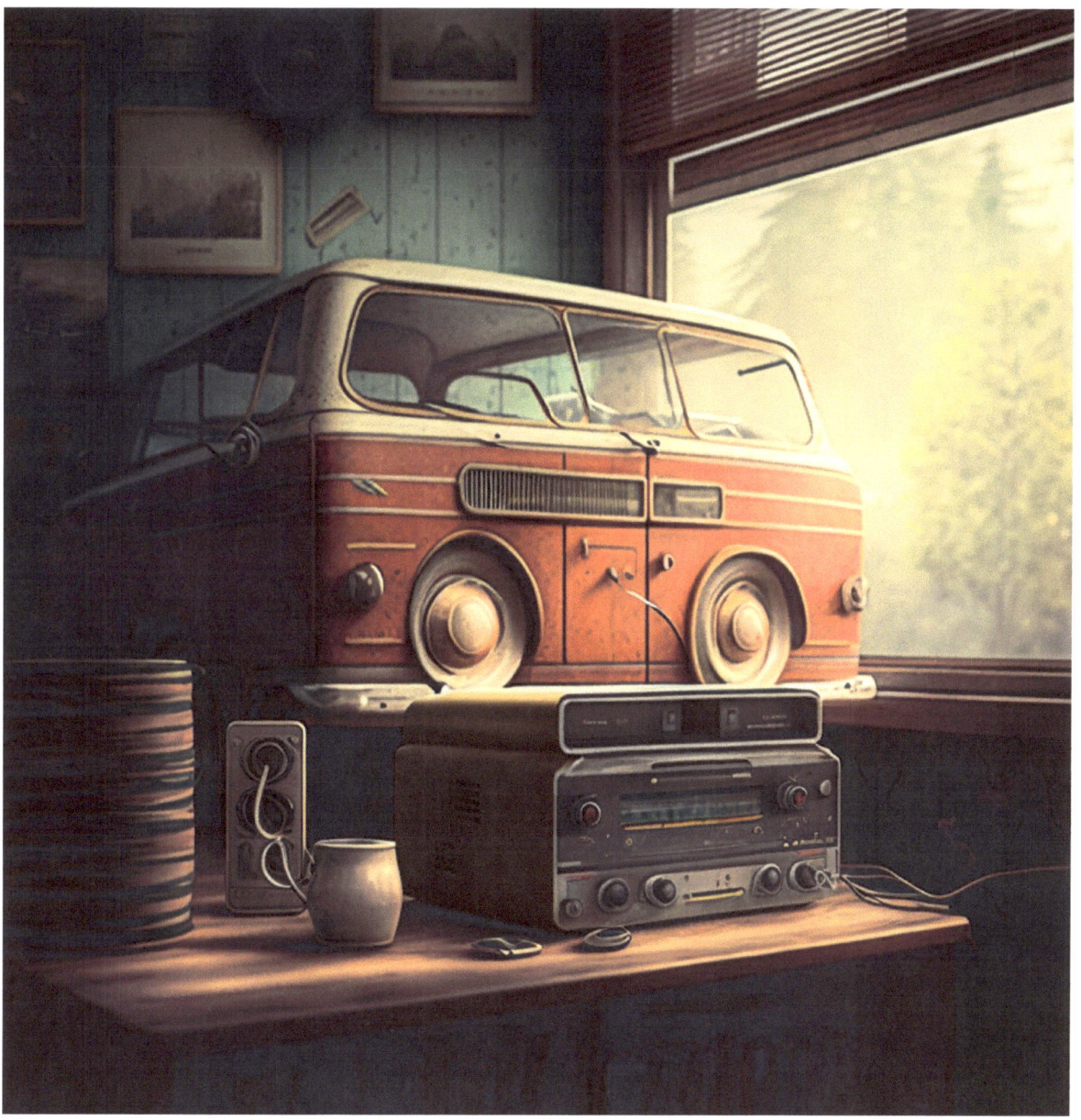

Prompt: Design a piece that evokes a sense of wonder and awe.

Output:

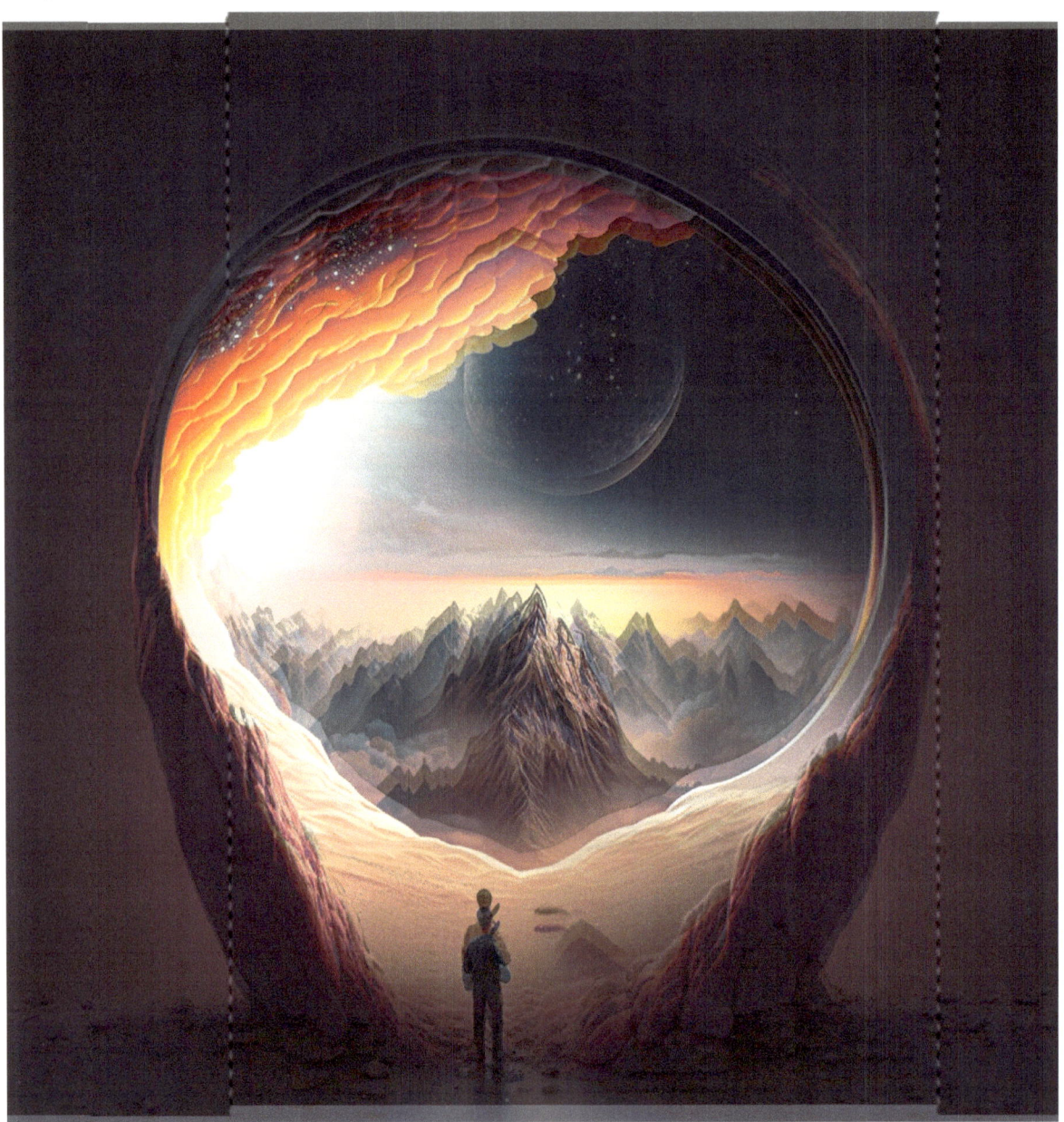

Prompt: Generate an image that conveys a sense of adventure and excitement.

Output:

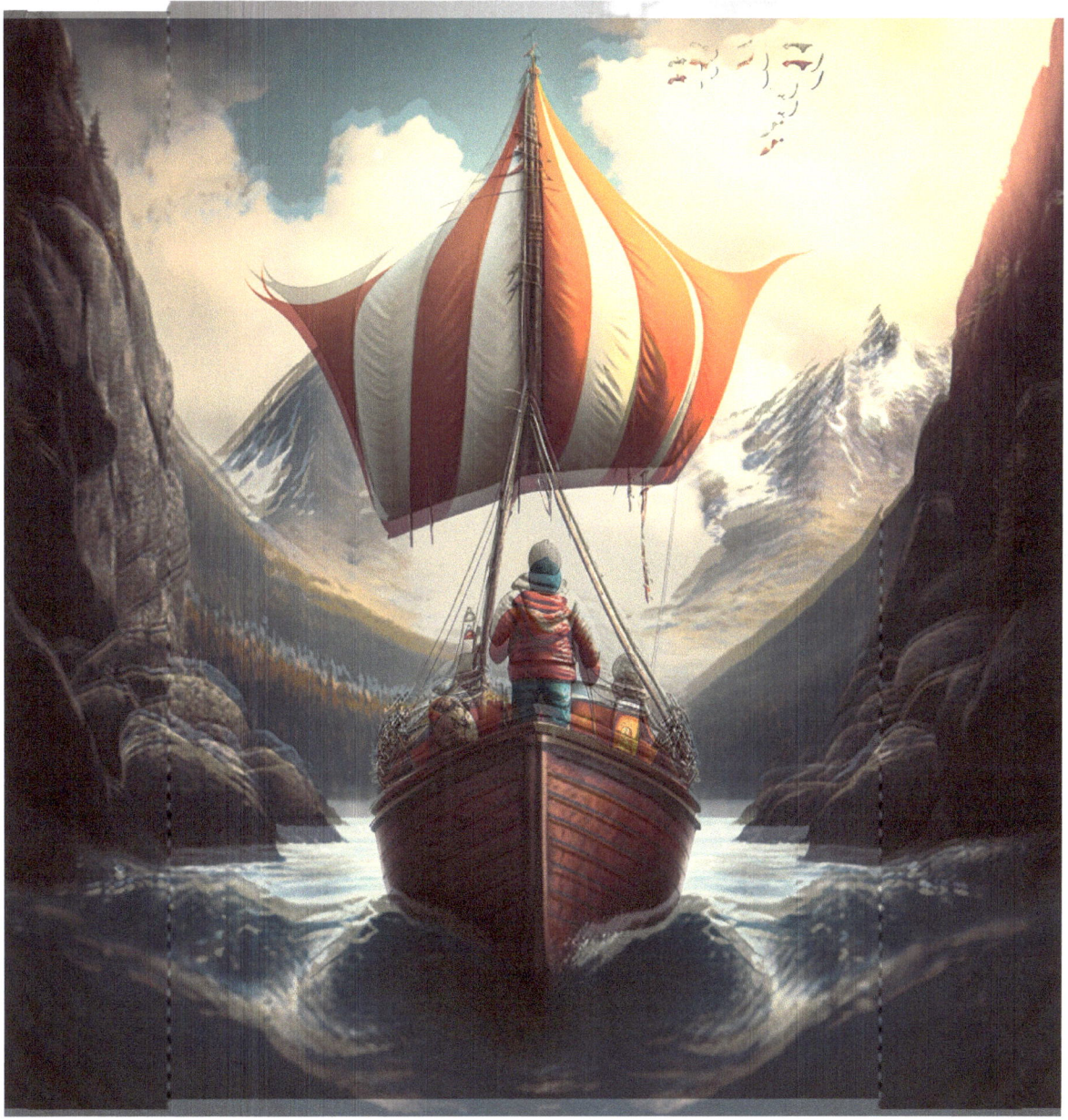

Prompt: Generate an artwork that conveys a sense of strength and power.

Output:

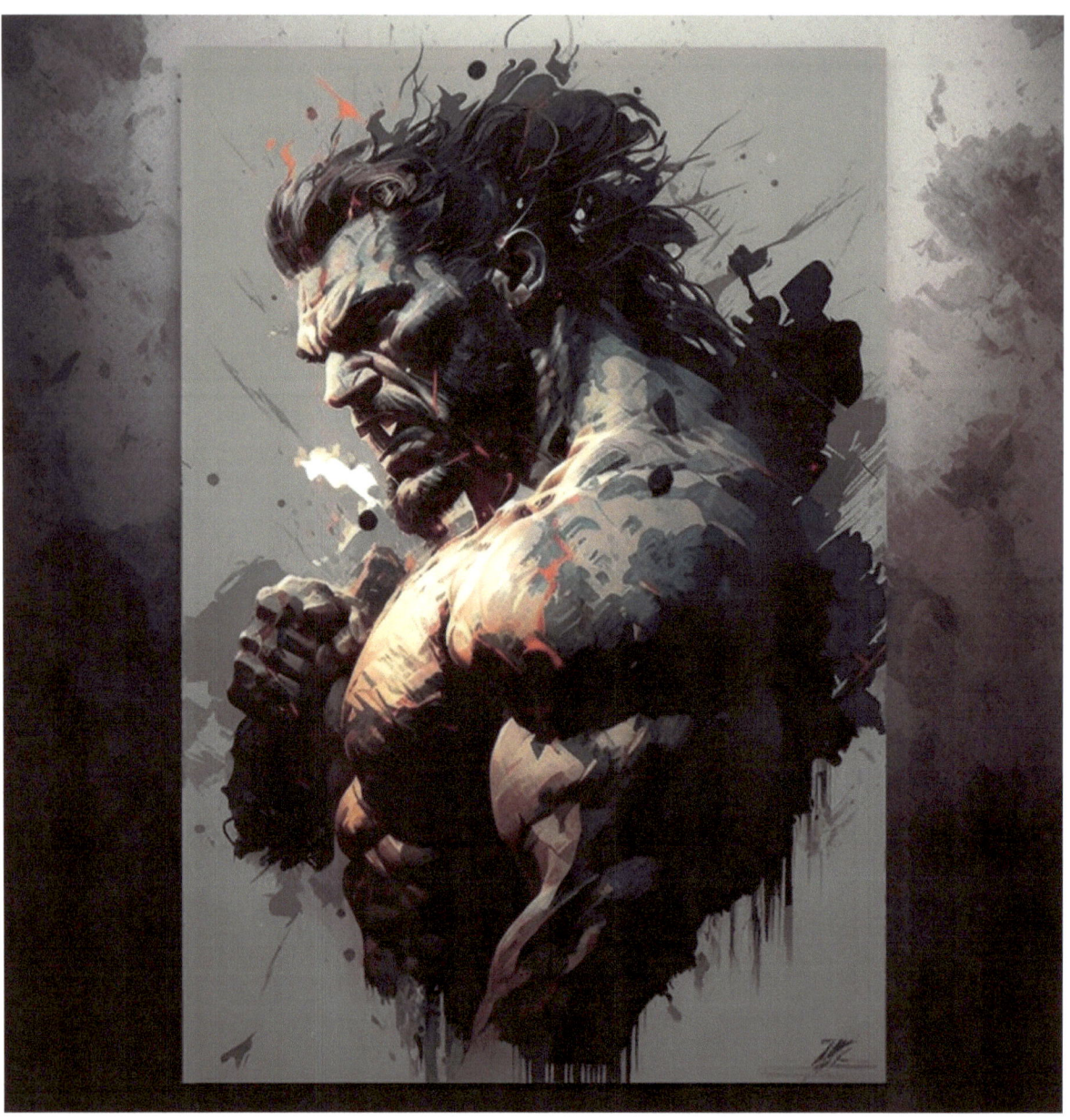

Randomized prompts

Prompt: Generate an image that combines elements of the ocean and outer space.

Output:

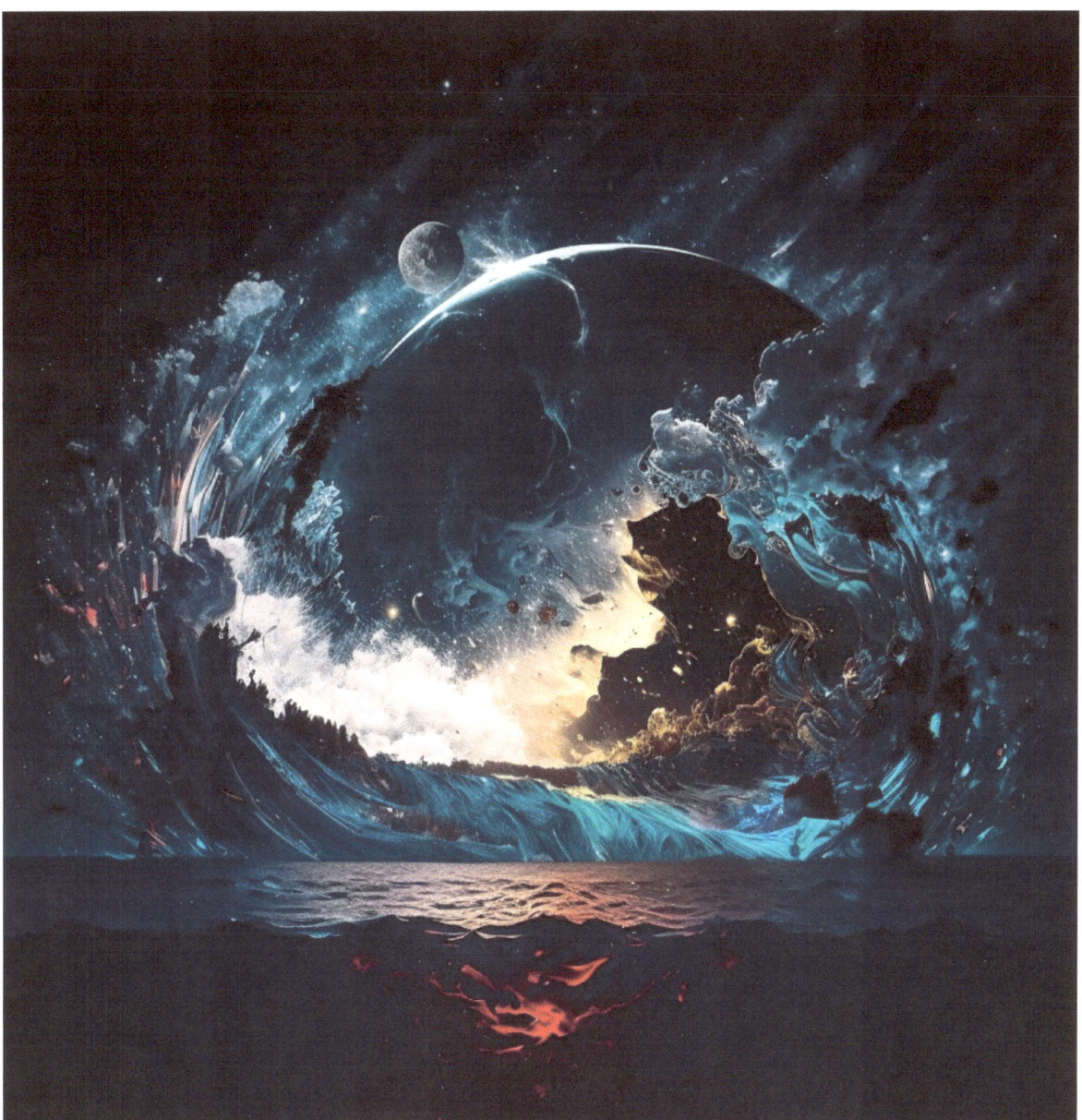

Prompt: Generate an image that combines elements of nature and technology.

Output:

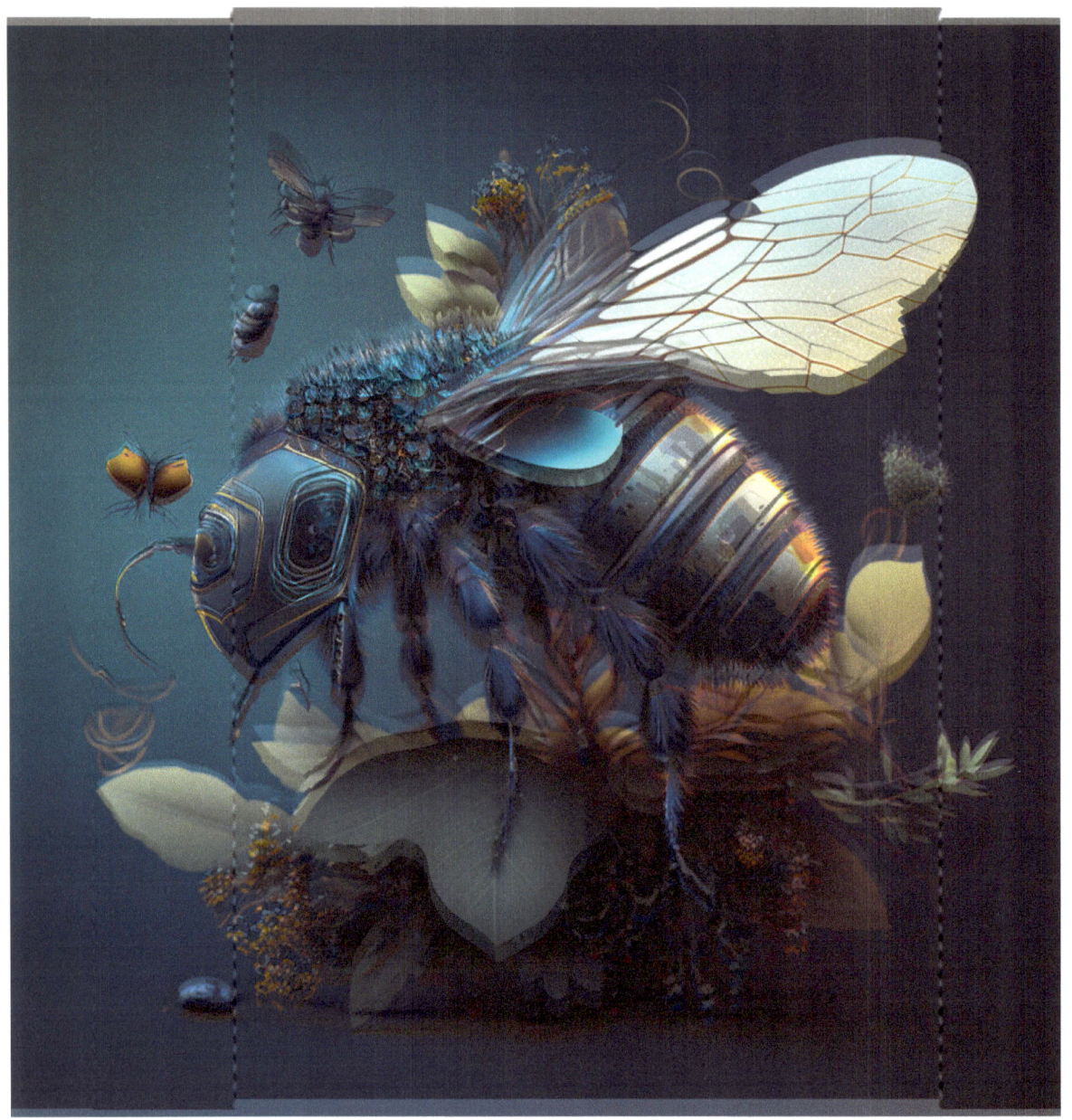

Prompt: Create a surreal landscape with floating islands and glowing mushrooms.

Output:

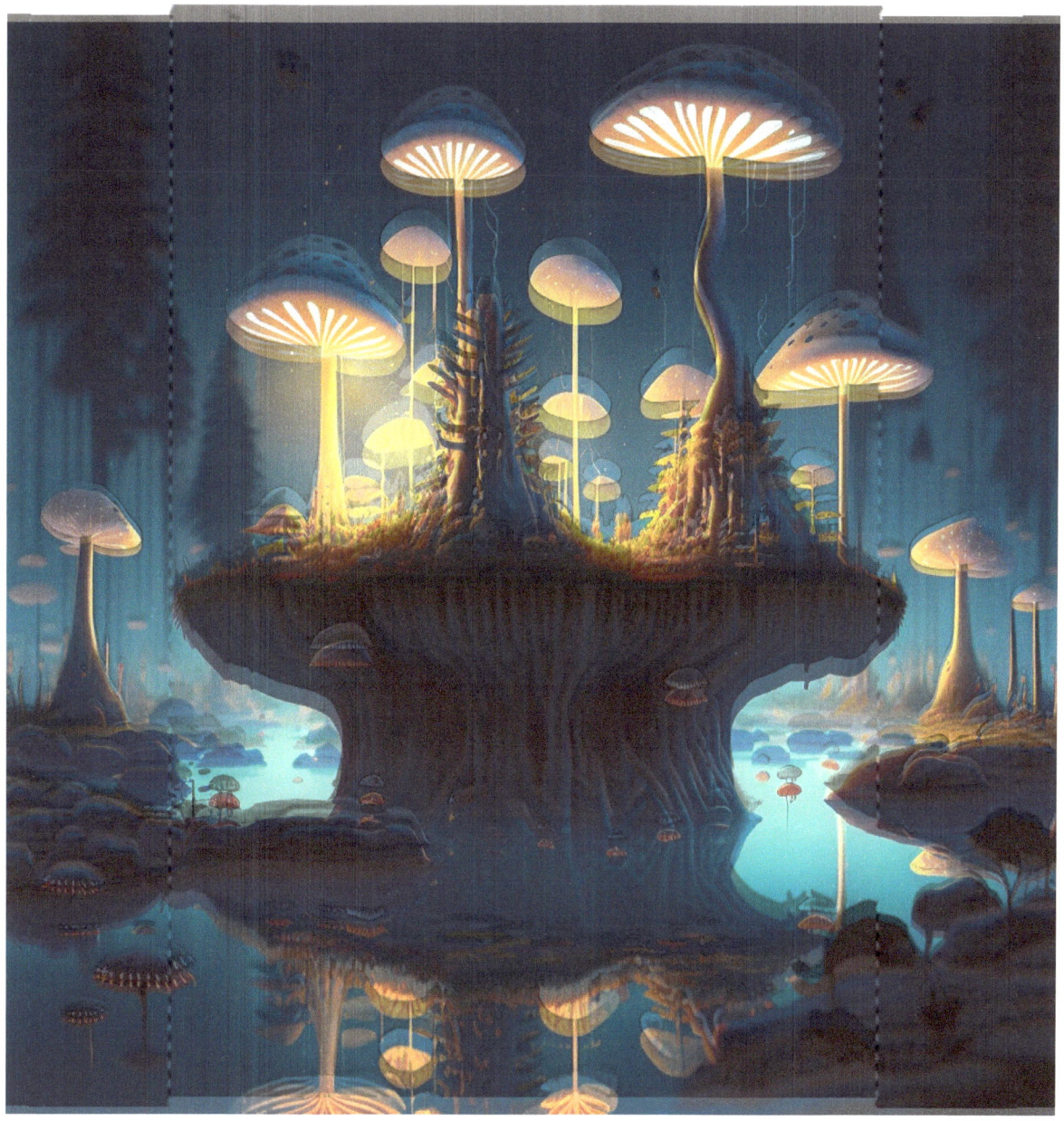

Prompt: Create an abstract image that incorporates geometric shapes and neon colours.

Output:

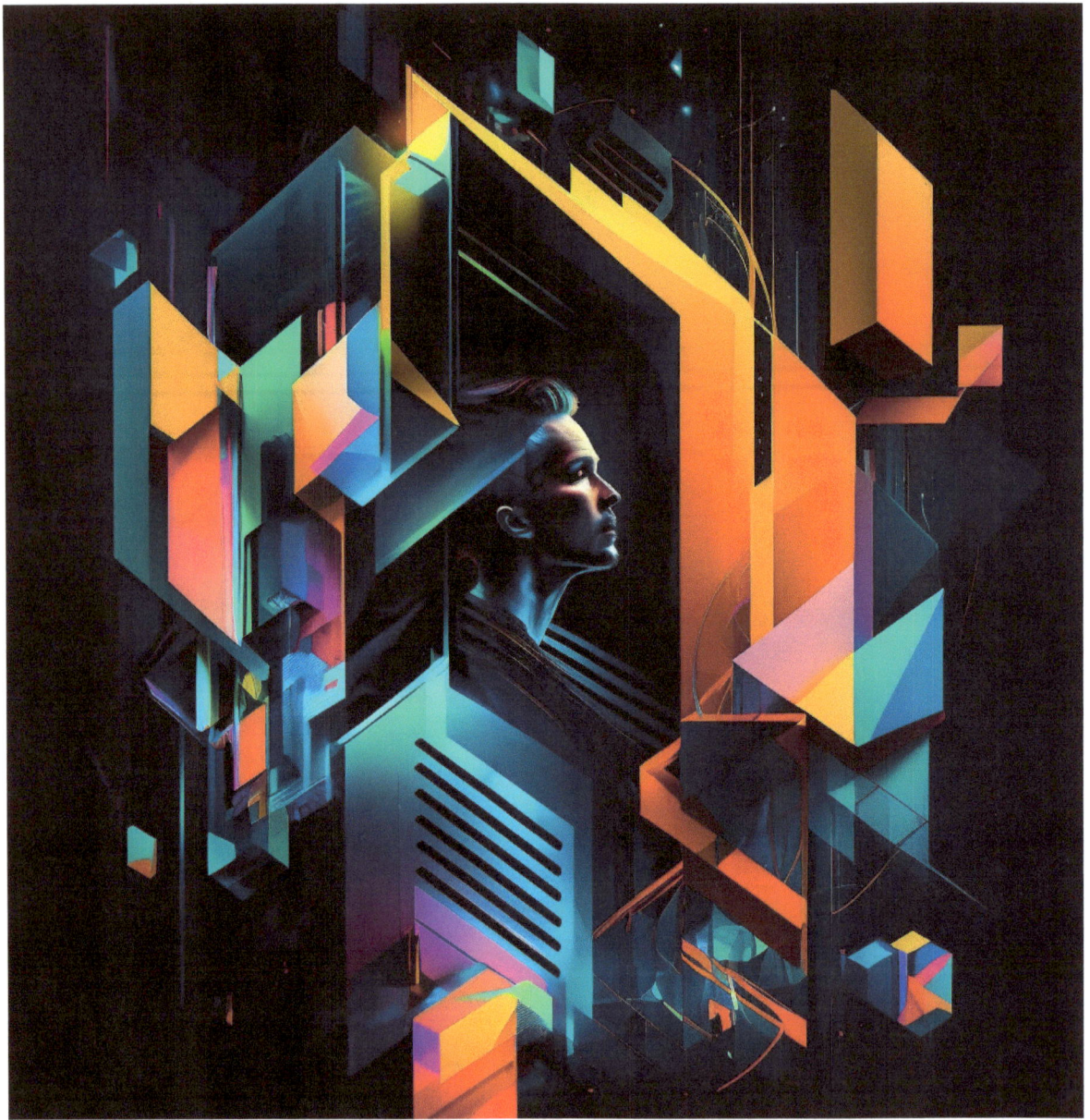

Online tools and resources for creating AI-generated art

If you're interested in creating your own AI-generated art, there are a variety of online tools and resources available to help you get started. Here are a few options:

1. **Artbreeder** - This platform allows users to combine and evolve different images to create unique and stunning artwork. It uses GANs to generate new images based on user input.

2. **Deep Dream Generator** - This tool uses Google's DeepDream algorithm to generate psychedelic and surreal images. Users can upload their own images and customize the parameters to create unique works of art.

3. **Runway ML** - This is a more advanced platform that allows users to create custom AI models for generating art. It requires some programming knowledge but can lead to more personalized and sophisticated results.

4. **NeuralStyle.art** - This tool uses neural style transfer to apply the style of one image to another. Users can upload their own images and select a style to create unique and interesting artworks.

5. **Google's Quick, Draw!** - This is a fun and interactive tool that uses machine learning to recognize and categorize drawings. Users can draw simple sketches and see how the AI model interprets their drawings.

These are just a few examples of the many online tools and resources available for creating AI-generated art. Whether you're a beginner or an advanced user, there's something out there for everyone to experiment with and create their own unique works of art. I have provided links to some of the most populate AI art generation tools at the end of this book.

How to get started with creating your own AI-generated art

If you're interested in creating your own AI-generated art, here are some steps to help you get started:

1. Familiarize yourself with the different types of AI algorithms used in art generation, such as GANs, style transfer, and neural networks. This will help you understand the underlying principles of how these algorithms work and how they can be applied to create art.

2. Choose an online tool or platform to experiment with. There are many options available, such as Artbreeder, Deep Dream Generator, Runway ML, and NeuralStyle.art. Try out different tools to see which ones work best for you and your artistic goals.

3. Explore the different prompts and techniques used in AI-generated art. You can find prompts online or come up with your own based on your artistic vision. Experiment with different techniques, such as adjusting parameters, combining images, and applying different styles.

4. Start with simple projects and gradually increase the complexity. This will help you build your skills and confidence as you become more comfortable with the tools and techniques.

5. Collaborate with other artists and share your work online. There is a vibrant community of AI-generated artists who are passionate about sharing their work and collaborating with others. Join online communities, attend events, and share your work to get feedback and connect with other artists.

Creating AI-generated art can be a fun and rewarding experience, even for those with little to no artistic background. With the right tools and resources, anyone can experiment with AI-generated art and create their own unique works of art.

Tips and tricks for success

1. Start with simple prompts and techniques: Don't overwhelm yourself by starting with complex prompts and techniques. Begin with simple projects and gradually increase the complexity as you become more familiar with the tools and techniques.

2. Experiment with different parameters: Adjusting parameters is one of the key ways to generate different variations of your AI-generated art. Experiment with different parameter settings to achieve different effects and styles.

3. Combine multiple images: Combining multiple images is a powerful technique for creating complex and unique art. Experiment with combining different images and see what interesting and unexpected results you can achieve.

4. Take breaks: Creating AI-generated art can be a time-consuming process. Take breaks when you need to, and come back to your project with fresh eyes.

5. Share your work and seek feedback: Share your work online and in online communities to get feedback from others. This will help you improve your skills and learn new techniques.

6. Don't be afraid to make mistakes: Making mistakes is a natural part of the creative process. Don't be afraid to try new things and experiment with different techniques, even if you're not sure they will work.

7. Have fun: Most importantly, have fun! Creating AI-generated art is a fun and rewarding experience, and the more you enjoy the process, the more successful you are likely to be.

8 CHALLENGES AND OPPORTUNITIES

There are several challenges and opportunities in the field of AI art:

Challenges:

1. Lack of creativity: AI-generated art is often criticized for being repetitive and lacking creativity. Many argue that AI systems lack the human ability to think outside the box and come up with truly unique and innovative ideas.

2. Ethics and bias: AI systems can be biased based on the data they are trained on, which can result in discriminatory or offensive art. It's important to be aware of the ethical implications of AI-generated art and take steps to prevent bias and discrimination.

3. Technical limitations: AI-generated art is limited by the capabilities of the AI system and the quality of the input data. As AI technology continues to evolve, these limitations are likely to become less significant, but they are still a challenge for artists working with AI.

Opportunities:

1. New forms of expression: AI-generated art presents new opportunities for artists to express themselves and create unique and innovative works of art that would not be possible without AI technology.

2. Automation and efficiency: AI technology can automate certain tasks in the creative process, such as generating patterns or colour schemes, freeing up time for artists to focus on other aspects of their work.

3. Collaboration: AI-generated art can be used as a tool for collaboration between artists and AI systems, allowing for new forms of creativity and experimentation.

4. Accessibility: AI-generated art has the potential to make art more accessible to people who may not have had the opportunity or resources to pursue traditional forms of art. With the help of AI technology, anyone can create art, regardless of their artistic background or training.

While there are certainly challenges associated with AI-generated art, there are also exciting opportunities for artists to explore and push the boundaries of traditional art forms.

Ethical concerns around AI-generated art

As with any emerging technology, there are ethical concerns surrounding AI-generated art. Here are some key ethical considerations:

1. Bias and discrimination: AI systems can be trained on biased or discriminatory data, resulting in AI-generated art that perpetuates or amplifies harmful stereotypes and biases. It's important for artists and AI developers to be aware of this potential and take steps to prevent it.

2. Ownership and copyright: AI-generated art raises questions about ownership and copyright. Who owns the rights to AI-generated art: the artist, the AI system, or the owner of the data used to train the AI? These questions are still being debated and will likely require new legal frameworks to address.

3. Authenticity and originality: AI-generated art challenges traditional notions of authenticity and originality. Some argue that AI-generated art is not truly original, as it is created using algorithms and pre-existing data. Others argue that AI-generated art can be just as authentic and original as traditional art.

4. Privacy and consent: AI systems can collect and analyze large amounts of data, including personal information, to create art. It's important for artists and AI developers to obtain consent from individuals whose data is being used and to ensure that their privacy is protected.

5. Social and cultural impact: AI-generated art has the potential to impact social and cultural norms and values. It's important to consider the potential impact of AI-generated art on society and to use the technology responsibly.

It is important for artists and AI developers to be aware of the potential ethical concerns associated with AI-generated art and to take steps to mitigate these concerns. This includes being transparent about the data used to train AI systems, obtaining consent from individuals whose data is being used, and considering the potential impact of AI-generated art on society and culture.

Potential future developments in the field

The field of AI-generated art is constantly evolving, and there are several potential future developments to look out for. Some of these include:

1. Improved Algorithms: One of the most promising areas of development is the continued improvement of algorithms used for generating art. As machine learning algorithms become more sophisticated, the quality of AI-generated art is likely to improve as well.

2. Increased Creativity: Another exciting development is the potential for AI to become more creative. Researchers are exploring ways to train algorithms to be more imaginative and to generate truly unique and original artworks.

3. Collaboration between Humans and Machines: As AI-generated art becomes more common, there is a growing interest in exploring ways for humans and machines to collaborate on artistic projects. This could lead to new forms of creative expression that would not be possible with either humans or machines working alone.

4. Interactive Art Installations: AI-generated art is already being used in interactive art installations that allow viewers to participate in the creation of the artwork. As this technology becomes more advanced, we can expect to see even more immersive and interactive art experiences.

5. Impact on the Art Market: AI-generated art has already had a significant impact on the art market, with some AI-generated artworks selling for millions of dollars. As the quality of AI-generated art continues to improve, it is likely to have an even greater impact on the art world.

6. Ethical Considerations: As AI-generated art becomes more prevalent, there are important ethical considerations to take into account. These include questions around ownership of the artwork, transparency around how the artwork was created, and concerns around the potential for AI-generated art to be used for nefarious purposes.

The potential for AI-generated art is vast, and we are likely to see continued growth and development in this field in the years to come.

How AI-generated art is changing the creative landscape

AI-generated art is changing the creative landscape in several ways. First, it is providing artists with new tools and techniques for creating artworks that were previously impossible or difficult to achieve. AI-generated art has opened up new possibilities for artists to explore and experiment with different styles, techniques, and mediums. Second, it is challenging traditional notions of authorship and originality. AI-generated artworks are often created collaboratively between the artist and the machine, blurring the lines between human and machine creativity. Third, it is democratizing access to art creation and consumption. AI-generated art tools and resources are becoming more accessible and affordable, allowing people with little or no artistic background to create and enjoy art.

AI-generated art is also changing the way we think about the role of technology in art. It is no longer just a tool for enhancing or supporting artistic expression, but rather a co-creator in the creative process. This raises important questions about the relationship between art and technology, and how we define creativity and artistic expression in the digital age.

Moreover, AI-generated art is changing the way we consume and appreciate art. It is challenging traditional notions of aesthetics and beauty, and introducing new forms of art that are often surreal, abstract, or unconventional. AI-generated art is also creating new opportunities for art to be integrated into different domains, such as design, advertising, and entertainment.

AI-generated art is a rapidly evolving field that is changing the creative landscape in exciting and unexpected ways. It is opening up new opportunities for artists, challenging traditional notions of creativity, and transforming the way we consume and appreciate art.

9 CONCLUSION

The potential of AI-generated art

The potential of AI-generated art is immense, and it is only just beginning to be explored. One of the most exciting aspects of AI-generated art is its ability to break down traditional barriers to creativity. With AI, artists and designers can explore new ideas, styles, and forms that would have been impossible without this technology. Additionally, AI-generated art has the potential to democratize creativity, allowing people with no formal artistic training to express themselves in new and exciting ways.

Another significant potential of AI-generated art is its ability to create works that are entirely unique and unpredictable. Because AI algorithms can create and combine ideas in novel ways, the resulting art can be surprising, beautiful, and thought-provoking. This unpredictability is part of what makes AI-generated art so exciting; it provides a sense of exploration and discovery that can be hard to find in traditional artistic mediums.

Furthermore, AI-generated art has the potential to revolutionize the art world by challenging our concepts of authorship and originality. As algorithms become more sophisticated, the line between human and machine-generated art may begin to blur. This raises important questions about the nature of creativity and what it means to be an artist. As AI-generated art continues to develop, we may need to reconsider our definitions of art, authorship, and creativity.

The potential of AI-generated art is vast and exciting, and we have only just scratched the surface of what this technology can do. From democratizing creativity to challenging our concepts of authorship and originality, AI-generated art is set to revolutionize the art world in ways we are only beginning to understand.

Key takeaways and final thoughts

One of the key takeaways from this book is the importance of prompt engineering in generating high-quality AI-generated art. By carefully selecting and designing prompts, artists can guide the AI algorithms towards producing desired outcomes that align with their artistic vision. Additionally, experimentation and exploration are crucial in discovering new possibilities and pushing the limits of what AI-generated art can achieve.

It is also worth considering the ethical implications of AI-generated art. As AI continues to grow and develop, it is important to ensure that it is used ethically and responsibly. This includes considerations such as ensuring that AI-generated art is not used to plagiarize or infringe upon the intellectual property of other artists, as well as protecting against the use of AI-generated art for malicious purposes.

Overall, the potential of AI-generated art is vast and exciting. As technology continues to evolve and improve, we can expect to see even more ground-breaking and innovative developments in this field. AI-generated art has the potential to transform the creative landscape, offering new possibilities for expression, experimentation, and artistic exploration.

10 EXPLORING FURTHER: ADDITIONAL RESOURCES FOR AI-GENERATED ART

Additional resources

Here is a list of some popular websites that allow users to generate AI art:

1. Deep Dream Generator - https://deepdreamgenerator.com/
2. ArtBreeder - https://www.artbreeder.com/
3. Runway ML - https://runwayml.com/
4. MidJourney - https://www.midjourney.com/
5. GANbreeder - https://ganbreeder.app/
6. NeuralStyle.art - https://neuralstyle.art/
7. Artisto - https://artisto.net/
8. Prisma - https://prisma-ai.com/
9. ArtEngine - https://www.artengine.ai/
10. PaintsChainer - https://paintschainer.preferred.tech/

These websites use a variety of AI algorithms, including GANs, neural networks, and style transfer to generate unique and captivating artworks based on user inputs, such as images or text prompts. Users can experiment with various styles, settings, and parameters to create their own personalized AI-generated art.

Go and have fun, your only limit is your imagination.

ABOUT THE AUTHOR

Field Du Boulay has been a software engineer and web applications developer for 25 years. He wrote his first webpage in 1998 after coming across an article during his lunch hour which discussed this new thing called the world wide web and how HTML was used to build and connect webpages and build entire websites. He immediately went out to his local bookshop and purchased a book on HTML and threw himself into learning everything he could about programming websites.

He has worked in diverse industries from television to law and is currently a lead developer for a well-known web development agency.

Field lives and works in London and is married with two children

www.ingramcontent.com/pod-product-compliance
Lightning Source LLC
Chambersburg PA
CBHW051954210526
45473CB00029B/813